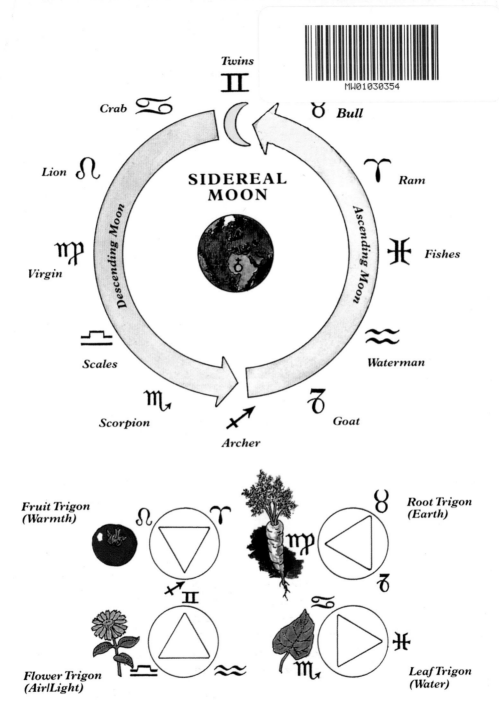

Twins

Crab

Bull

Lion

Ram

SIDEREAL
MOON

Descending Moon

Ascending Moon

Virgin

Fishes

Waterman

Scales

Scorpion

Goat

Archer

Fruit Trigon
(Warmth)

Root Trigon
(Earth)

Flower Trigon
(Air/Light)

Leaf Trigon
(Water)

MARIA THUN

Gardening for Life – The Biodynamic Way

a practical introduction to a new art of
gardening, sowing, planting, harvesting

Compiled for gardeners by
Angelika Throll-Keller

Hawthorn Press

English edition copyright © 1999 Hawthorn Press,
Hawthorn House, 1 Lansdown Lane, Stroud, Gloucestershire, GL5 1BJ, UK
Tel: (01453) 757040 Fax: (01453) 751138
E-mail: info@hawthornpress.com
Website: **www.hawthornpress.com**

Translated and edited by Matthew Barton
Cover design by Patrick Roe, Southgate Solutions Ltd
Typeset at Hawthorn Press by Jim Sweeney
Printed in China by Everbest Printing Company
Reprinted 2004, 2007, 2009, 2012

Printed on paper sourced from sustainable forest stock.

Grateful acknowledgements for help with this book to: Ian Bailey, Karen Herms, Bernard Jarman and Jessica Standing.

A catalogue record of this book is available from the British Library Cataloguing in Publication Data

ISBN 978-1-869890-32-2

CONTENTS

5

**Grain field-trials
are harvested with a
combine harvester,
and differences in
bread-quality are
later compared after
baking.**

CONTENTS

FOREWORD

Much of this book has previously appeared in a variety of periodicals and articles, or in self-published booklets. While it gives an overview of our work, themes have been selected which focus particularly on questions of small-scale cultivation.

Our research and experiments are based on bio-dynamic methods, developed from the recommendations and ideas which Rudolf Steiner presented in his 1924 course of eight lectures for farmers and gardeners. This approach pre-dates other alternative cultivation methods which have since been tried out. It has been compared with other organic or conventional methods in many tests and trials. The 'preparations' mentioned at many places in the book, as well as the process of making ashes from insect pests and weeds (so-called 'peppers') derive from Rudolf Steiner's recommendations.

Long years of research have enabled us to deepen, expand and refine our understanding of cosmic influences on plant growth, an aspect which can be of great use to the practical gardener.

Co-worker analysing plant-oil. The effects of different cultivation methods on oil-bearing plants are shown clearly through plant-oil extraction.

Maria Thun

THE ZODIAC

From our perspective on earth, the sun passes in front of each of the twelve particular constellation regions of the zodiac in the course of a year. The moon and all the planets pass only in front of these particular constellations. As they do so, they mediate impulses to the earth (see drawing on inside flap of cover).

The shape and form of the plant can make visible the influences issuing from these heavenly bodies. In the formation of nutritional substance too, such as proteins, fats, carbohydrates and salts, it responds to the stimulus and growth-impulse of cosmic rhythms.

We ascertained the 'cusps' or transitional points from one constellation to another by sowing large numbers of plants at hourly intervals. This required a great deal of work, but the plants clearly showed us how the influences affecting them changed at each step of the way. We also noted shifts in time related to the moon being closer (perigee) or further (apogee) from the earth, which have to be worked out each year anew for our *Sowing and Planting Calendar.*

At present, the sun stands in the constellations of the zodiac at the following times:[2]

- Fishes: 11 March - 17 April
- Ram: 18 April - 12 May
- Bull: 13 May - 19 June
- Twins: 20 June - 9 August
- Crab: 19 July - 9 August
- Lion: 10 August - 14 September
- Virgin: 15 September - 31 October
- Scales: 1 November - 18 November
- Scorpion: 19 November - 18 December
- Archer: 19 December - 17 January
- Goat: 18 January - 13 February
- Waterman: 14 February - 10 March

COSMIC RELATIONSHIPS

It was nearly 50 years ago that Rudolf Steiner's booklet, *Practical Training in Thinking*,[3] first encouraged us to observe plants in a new and unusual way. We soon found noticeable differences despite the same cultivation and conditions – such as parent stock, seed, germination and manuring. One plot or bed often produced a higher yield than another of the same size. Since both had been cultivated in the same way, the cause of the difference could not lie in – let us call it the 'spatial' realm – but in the 'temporal'. This was the starting-point for the research whose results are summarized in this book.

We know that all organic processes on earth take place within a sequence of time. Many such sequences recur in a continual rhythm. The best-known example is the rhythm of night and day, which calls forth great changes in our consciousness (waking, sleeping, dreaming).

The cosmic aspect of each sowing day is demonstrated in the cauliflower's 'fruit' formation: those sown on 'leaf days (left and right) form firm heads, while those sown on 'flower' days (middle) are very loose and quickly go to seed.

10

COSMIC RELATIONSHIPS

The day-night rhythm comes about as a result of the earth's orbit around its own axis. Day holds sway on the face of the earth turned towards the sun, while on the other side is night.

The cycle of the year is also a continually recurring rhythm. In the course of a year the earth circles the sun. At the beginning of January it is closer to the sun, then further away at the beginning of July.

The alternation of the seasons – spring, summer, autumn, winter – arises through the axis tilt of the earth. Since the earth's rotational axis is not vertical, but tilted at about 66 degrees, the poles are plunged into total darkness in winter and flooded in uninterrupted daylight in summer. Spring and autumn are more balanced, transitional periods. At the equator on the other hand, day and night are the same length all through the year – 12 unvarying hours of each.

Besides the seasons, which are determined by the earth's relationship to the sun, life-processes on earth are also influenced by the rhythms of the planets – Mercury, Venus, Mars, Jupiter, Saturn, Uranus, Neptune, Pluto, and the moon. Plants are able to make visible the impulses and influences which emanate from the planets, sun and moon (for example, in the 'head' of a lettuce) in their shape and structure. Protein-, fat-, carbohydrate - and salt - content are also affected.

As we proceeded with our research one basic law became increasingly apparent: the constellations of the zodiac are of great importance for plant growth. They work through sun, moon and the planets, which in turn pass on their own properties to the plant through the classical elements of warmth, light/air, water and earth.

The sowing time, when the seed enters the earth, exerts the strongest influence. Planting-out time, when the plant is moved and replanted, is also highly significant. It can either enhance or weaken the impulse which the seed received at sowing time.

It is also important to choose a good time for preparing the soil, since this opens up the earth to planetary and zodiac influences, and can likewise enhance growth if the moment is favourable.

Harvest time is also decisive. For example, if one chooses a poor time to harvest seeds or parts of plants which are to be used for sowing or propagation, the following year's crop will be largely weak and sickly. Fruits and vegetables will rot more easily in storage if they have been harvested at a time of unfavourable cosmic conditions. You can read more about these 'favourable' times on pages 18-31, where we have summarized the results of our research on individual

Onions in May, from the previous year's September harvest. The onions harvested on leaf days (left-hand side of photo, marked AK) are rotting. Those harvested on fruit and flower days (marked WK and LK) are sprouting. Only those harvested on root days (marked EK) are still as firm as they were in September, and remain so at least until the following August.

plant species. On pages 95 onwards you can find further results.

The sidereal moon

The moon orbits the earth once every 27.3 days. During this orbit it passes through the twelve zodiac regions. Every two to four days it stands in a new constellation, mediating to the earth through the classical elements (warmth, light/air, water, earth) the forces of that constellation as it passes in front of it. (See table on page 13 and the drawing on the cover's inside flap.)

Each constellation is one of a trigon of three similar constellations. Since there are twelve constellations in the zodiac, we get four such trigons. To each is assigned one of the classical elements (see drawing on page 1).

From the beginning we also noticed that weather observations were a necessary parts of our plant trials, and clear patterns soon became apparent. Sowing days which were favourable for leaf growth always tended to be damp. These 'leaf days' had the greatest moisture and the highest rainfall of the month. Our weather observations also demonstrated that the classical elements should be assigned to different parts of the plant (see table).

As the moon passes every two to four days from one constellation to another, the character of cosmic influence changes. ('Water', for example, changes after two to four days to 'warmth', as can be seen from the table.) Roughly every nine days the moon reaches a constellation of the same trigon again, and the original impulse or influence recurs. By hoeing and silica spraying, which we carry out in the trigon rhythm most favourable to the particular type of plant, we keep renewing the impulse which the seed originally received at sowing.

These basic laws and regularities do not always apply however. Planetary oppositions and certain 'trigon' positions can alter the usual influence, and activate different elements from that mediated by the moon on the day in question. Multiple conjunctions exert a negative effect.

In the table below we have summarized the regularities which became apparent through our plant-trials and weather observations:

zodiac sign	element	microclimate	plant organ
Fishes	water	moist	leaf
Ram	warmth	warm	fruit
Bull	earth	cool/cold	root
Twins	air/light	airy/light	flower
Crab	water	moist	leaf
Lion	warmth	warm	fruit, seed
Virgin	earth	cool/cold	root
Scales	air/light	airy/light	flower
Scorpion	water	moist	leaf
Archer	warmth	warm	fruit
Goat	earth	cool/cold	root
Waterman	air/light	airy/light	flower

The planetary positions represented here can alter the influence normally exerted on plants by the zodiac sign in which the moon stands. (The earth ♄ ♅ is always depicted at the centre of the outer circle.)

Top: Planetary opposition of Mars (left) and sun (right).
Middle: Trine position of Mercury (left) and Jupiter (right).
Bottom: Conjunction of Saturn (far left) and Venus (left).

For example, negative effects arise on days when the moon crosses the path (ecliptic) of the earth in either an upward or downward direction. These negative effects are intensified when the moon and planets meet one another at their paths' crossing points (called nodes). Eclipses and partial eclipses arise, in which the effect of the more distant planet is interrupted or altered by the nearer one. Such times are unsuitable for sowing or harvesting.

This is only a brief resumé of the factors playing in to our calculations.

There is no need to be well-versed in astronomy to garden in accordance with these sowing recommendations.

Negative influences on plants come about, for example, on days when the paths of two planets cross (nodes), when eclipses are likely. Sowing should be avoided on such days.

We take all the possible variations and negative effects into account in our *Sowing and Planting Calendar* which is published each year for the year ahead.

The planets and their effect on the earth

Like the sun and the moon, the planets also influence the weather, using the classical elements of warmth, earth, air/light and water to mediate their influence on the earth.

We have ascertained the following relationships:

of its warming influence is apparent. On the contrary, it can exert a cooling influence instead. When Mercury passes through a 'watery' constellation like Scorpion, its warming influence can produce showers.

When Venus passes in front of an air/light constellation such as Scales, we are likely to get clear blue skies, long periods of sunshine and clear atmosphere. But if it is in an earth sign,

planets* and sun	element	constellation
Saturn, Mercury, Pluto	warmth	Ram, Lion, Archer
Sun	earth	Bull, Virgin, Goat
Jupiter, Venus, Uranus	air/light	Twins, Scales, Waterman
Moon, Mars, Neptune	water	Crab, Scorpion, Fishes

* the word planet literally means 'wanderer' or a celestial body which moves, unlike the 'fixed stars'

When the planets pass in front of zodiac constellations of the same element, their effect is intensified. (For example: Mercury in Aries.) But when a planet is in a constellation which relates to a different element, the effect is either weakened or non-existent.

Here are just a few examples:
When a 'warmth' planet like Mercury passes through Ram, its effect is intensified; but when it is in Bull none

such as Virgo, it can produce cold nights and fog. In watery signs, Venus' air/light effect fails to come into its own.

When the moon, or planets which work through the watery element, pass across a region of the zodiac which also corresponds to water, there are likely to be periods of precipitation.

There are numerous other factors which exert an influence, such as

15

Kohlrabi (White Roggli's variety).

Far left: Sown on leaf days, gently rounded, very delicate kohlrabis are produced.
Second from left: Sown on fruit days, they swell into 'fruits' which easily form a tough husk.
Third from left: Sown on root days, they develop scabs and tend to become woody.
Right: Sown on flower days, they develop 'fruits' which start shooting into flower and seed.

These kohlrabis were sown when the moon was in perigee (closest to the earth). Of each group of 50 plants, 25 produced these 'fruits'.

planetary oppositions to one another or the sun, which usually produce growth-enhancing conditions.

One can observe a relationship to electricity in Uranus, to magnetism in Neptune, and to volcanic activity in Pluto.

ABOUT THIS BOOK

In our experience, the effects of planets, zodiac constellations and other factors in the realm beyond the earth's atmosphere are extremely important for gardeners and farmers. Each year we produce *The Biodynamic Sowing and Planting Calendar,*[1] a little booklet in which you can find the favourable and unfavourable days (for that year) for sowing, planting and cultivation, as well as for harvesting and preserving.

Illustration shows a page from The Biodynamic Sowing and Planting Calendar.

January 2004

Date	*Const. of Moon*	*Other aspects*		*Moon Element*		*Parts of the plant enhanced by Moon or planets*	*Weather, etc.*
1 Thu	♈ 3h		☉-♐	Water/Warmth	SPT	Leaf to 2h, Fruit from 3h	
2 Fri	♈	☊20h		Warmth		Fruit to 18h and from 22h	St
3 Sat	♉ 4h	**Ag** 20h		Warmth/Earth		Fruit to 3h, Root 4h to 13h, Flower 14h to 23h	
4 Sun	♉			Earth		Root from 0h	Eq
5 Mon	♉			Earth		Root	
6 Tue	♊ 5h	⌒22h		Earth/Light		Root to 4h, Flower from 5h	♄
7 Wed	♊	Ⓟ16h		Light	Northern Planting Time	Flower	
8 Thu	♋ 12h			Light/Water		Flower to 11h, Leaf from 12h	
9 Fri	♋		△	Water		Leaf to 11h, Fruit from 12h	Eq
10 Sat	♌ 4h			Water/Warmth		Fruit	
11 Sun	♌			Warmth		Fruit	♄
12 Mon	♍ 21h			Warmth/Earth		Fruit to 20h, Root from 21h	
13 Tue	♍			Earth		Root	
14 Wed	♍			Earth		Root	St
15 Thu	♍			Earth		Root	♄
16 Fri	♎ 6h	☋21h		Earth/Light		Root to 5h, Flower from 6h to 19h	Vo
17 Sat	♏ 13h			Light/Water		Flower to 12h, Leaf from 13h	Tr St
18 Sun	♏		**☉-♑**	Water		Leaf	
19 Mon	♐ 15h	**Pg** 19h		Water		--------------------------------	
20 Tue	♐	◡6h	**△**	Warmth	Southern Planting Time	Leaf to 13h, Fruit from 14h	St
21 Wed	♑ 16h	●21h	△	Warmth/Earth		Flower from 15h, Root from 16h	St
22 Thu	♑		☿☍♄	Earth		--------------------------------	
23 Fri	♒ 15h			Earth/Light		Root from 3h to 14h, Flower from 15h	
24 Sat	♒			Light		Flower	
25 Sun	♓ 11h			Light/Water		Flower from 10h, Leaf from 11h	Tr St
26 Mon	♓		☿☋22h	Water		--------------------------------	Vo
27 Tue	♓			Water		Leaf from 5h	Tr
28 Wed	♈ 11h			Water/Warmth		Leaf to 10h, Fruit from 11h to 21h	♄
29 Thu	♈	☊ 22h	♀☍♃ △	Warmth		Fruit from 14h to 20h	
30 Fri	♉ 12h			Warmth/Earth		Fruit from 0h to 11h, Root from 12h	St
31 Sat	♉	**Ag** 14h		Earth		Root to 8h, Flower from 9h to 17h, Root from 18h	

Mercury	Venus	Mars	Jupiter	Saturn	Uranus	Neptune	Pluto
♐ 2♏ 12♐	♑ 11♒	♓	♌	♊	♒	♑	♏

SOWING

The moment at which the seed is entrusted to the earth has the strongest formative influence. To decide the best time for sowing, therefore, we must know what part of the plant we wish to harvest. If we are sowing carrot seed for instance, the root is of prime importance, so sowing should take place on a 'root-day' (see table on page **13,** and inside flap of back cover). Our long years of research have distinguished four broad categories of plants: root-plants, leaf-plants, flower-plants and fruit-plants.

If you can't find the plant you're looking for in this book, you can classify it yourself according to which part of it you want to harvest.

Plants sown on root-days

The main 'fruit' of such plants is formed in their roots. Among these belong celeriac, swede, carrots, parsnip, radish, beetroot, black salsify and root parsley. These vegetables produce the best yield, and store best, when sown on root days. The same is true of onions, potatoes and garlic.

Plants sown on leaf-days

To this group belong most of the cabbages, as well as kohlrabi and cauliflower, but not broccoli (which is a flower plant); also the lettuces, lamb's lettuce, endives, chicory, spinach, asparagus, fennel (and grass). Parsley and leaf herbs, which do not contain etheric oils, also belong here.

The time of sowing has the greatest effect on the future plant

18

Baskets of spinach; the plants sown on leaf days produce about 30% more than those sown on other days.

Beans belong to the fruit plants

Plants sown on fruit days

This group includes all the plants whose seed-fruits we harvest: beans, peas, lentils, soya, maize or sweetcorn, tomato and peppers, all the varieties of squash and pumpkin, as well as zucchini and cucumber. Also grains and cereals, whether sown in summer or winter.

Plants sown on flower days

To this group belong the plants which emphasize bloom and blossom: the flowers, bulb plants, broccoli, many medicinal plants, and the plants from which we make bio-dynamic compost 'preparations' (see page **41**). As well as sowing the seeds of such plants on flower days, one should also carry out any cultivation (hoeing etc.) on flower days too.

The seed

To harvest good seed it is important to pay special attention to quality. The seed must have the capacity to produce healthy growth without becoming susceptible to fungal infection, and have the strength to reach the fruiting and seed stage. Many of our edible plants form a fully-fledged 'organ' which, if we are not trying to grow new seed, we eat before any seed has formed.

If we want to harvest seed, we must be careful to take it from plants which have formed a particularly fine 'fruit'. Pictured here are a flowering radish (above) and a flowering broccoli (below).

THE SEED

**Growing your own seed –
lettuce for example**

1. Sowing is best done on a leaf
day.
2. All cultivation should be
done on leaf days, until a
good, firm head of lettuce is
produced.
3. Once the lettuce is ready for
harvesting, cultivation should
shift to fruit and fruit/seed
days, to enable the plant to
form strong, healthy seeds.
4. The seeds shouls be
harvested on a leaf day, which
will give the new lettuce plants
a boost in forming heads of
lettuce the following year.

For example: if we harvest seed
from a lettuce that did not previously
produce a good firm head, then the
plants which grow from this seed will
also fail to produce good heads of
lettuce. Sowing and cultivation of
lettuce are best done on leaf days.
Once a good head has developed, we
should shift cultivation to fruit and

fruit/seed days, to enable the plant to form strong, healthy seeds. But we harvest on a leaf day, since we want the seeds to produce good heads of lettuce the following year. The same applies to cauliflower and kohlrabi.

Many types of cabbage, carrots, beetroots, celeriac and fodder roots are kept in winter storage so that seed can be taken from them the following year. In spring they should be planted out and cultivated on fruit and fruit/seed days. The seeds are gathered on days corresponding to the part of the plant which will be harvested the following year - carrots on root days for example.

If beetroot, celeriac or turnip shoot into seed in the first year, their seed will not produce good 'root-fruits' the following year.

When fruit plants such as cucumber or tomato are sown for the purposes of seed harvesting, it is a good idea to carry out the sowing under a Lion influence, on fruit/seed days in other words. Further cultivation work can be done on fruit or fruit/seed days; and the seed should also be harvested on fruit/seed days (Lion).

If it proves impossible to sow on favourable days, then one should at least be careful to hoe on the right days. This will counteract the negative cosmic effect of the sowing day.

HOEING

Every time we work the soil - when hoeing or sowing for example - cosmic forces can enter the soil and exert either a positive or negative influence on plant growth. It is therefore very important to choose the best times for doing such work, according to the needs of individual plant species. If poor weather conditions hinder us from using the most favourable days, then we should wait for nine days or so until the moon passes in front

Hoeing should generally be done on the same days as are chosen for sowing.

of another constellation of the same trigon again.

If hoeing is carried out on unfavourable days, the positive effect of a good sowing or planting-out day is weakened.

So hoeing and cultivation should be carried out under the same influences that held sway at sowing. Lettuce, for example, is sown and also hoed on leaf days (see also the drawing on the inside flap of back cover).

We should hoe to a depth of no more than about 3 cm. This allows the high nitrogen content of the air to

23

enter the soil. After the proper autumn cultivation of the soil (see pp **33**) there will be enough bacteria in the earth to 'bind' the nitrogen to the earth element. Our experience has shown that hoeing produces a light 'manuring effect'.

One can also make use of the time of day when hoeing. In the morning the soil exhales, so if we hoe then we enable a soil that is too moist to breathe out some of its excess moisture. In the evening the soil inhales, and we can therefore help a soil that is too dry to breathe in moisture from the atmosphere at that time of day (see also pp **66**).

We found the following results when we tested the effects of hoeing:

- Hoeing on root days stimulates nitrogen binding.
- Hoeing on leaf days activates calcium processes.
- Hoeing on flower days enhances potassium and phosphor activity.
- Hoeing on fruit days activates sulphur processes.

Iceberg lettuce belongs to the leaf plants.

PLANTING OUT

Planting out is the term used for bringing young plants, shrubs etc. from one place to another and replanting them. The best time to do this is when the moon is 'descending' through the constellations (please do not confuse this with the waning moon - see drawing on page 1).

When is the moon descending? Orbiting the earth roughly once every 27 days, it ascends from its deepest point (in the region of Archer) to its highest point (Twins), then descends again.

Planting or planting out should always be done during the period of descending moon, since forces are then streaming into the lower parts of the plant. This leads to better and quicker root growth (see also drawing on page 1)

When it is descending the earth breathes in, and the sap-flow and forces of plants concentrate in their lower portion: this stimulates better and stronger root-growth, which is beneficial after planting out. When the moon is ascending the earth breathes out, and plant forces therefore become concentrated in their upper parts.

Besides being suitable for planting, the time of descending moon is very good for manuring fields and meadows, as well as for sowing leguminous plants for green manuring.

In the southern hemisphere these conditions are reversed.

If one chooses the leaf days of Crab or Scorpion - which fall within the descending moon period - for planting out leaf plants, this positive influence is further enhanced. The same applies to planting out root plants during the root days of Virgin, or planting cucumber and tomato on the fruit/seed days of Lion.

For planting bulbs we recommend choosing a flower day in November.

PLANTING OUT

Tulips (above) and Narcissi (below) are flower bulbs. It is good to plant these on a flower day in November when the moon is descending ('planting time').

PROPAGATION THROUGH CUTTINGS

Cuttings need to develop roots as quickly as possible, so one should plant them when the moon is descending (see previous chapter). The forces of growth concentrate on root formation at such times, so root growth is quicker and stronger. One should also take account of the 'type' of plant - 'leaf', 'flower' etc. Leaf scions of African violet produced the most blooms when planted with the moon in Twins (flower days).

Cuttings are taken with the moon ascending and stored in a cool room. One can wrap them in moistened paper and then plant them when the moon is descending again. Both cutting and planting times should relate to the plant 'type'.

Taking cuttings from Fuchsia

27

HARVESTING AND PRESERVING

The best days for harvesting are usually the ones which were best for sowing. In other words, 'flower' plants are best harvested on flower days, and 'fruit' plants on fruit days etc.

The leaf days are an exception, for vegetables harvested on those days do not keep or store well. Instead, flower or fruit days should be chosen - flower days are best for cabbage varieties.

Let me emphasize, though, that this only applies to vegetables for storing. Vegetables which go straight from the garden to the kitchen can be picked on any day - the fresher the better.

Fruit is best harvested during fruit days when the moon is ascending; and root vegetables on root days when it is in descending. We have seen why this is so in the previous chapter: during the period of descending, vitality and sap-flow stream downwards, and during ascending moon they rise upwards again. Strawberries are best picked on flower or fruit days, for they then taste better and stay fresh longer.

For kitchen and medicinal herbs we recommend the following: harvest leaf and flower herbs on flower days; seeds and wild fruits on fruit days; and roots on root days. This will ensure the best aroma and vitality. For preserving one should choose flower days.

Left: Choose fruit days for harvesting fruit. It is best if these lie within the period of ascending moon, since that is when plant forces rise more strongly into the upper portions of the plant. This also makes them considerably better for storing.

Right: Fruit harvest

In the morning plant forces stream from below upwards. This is therefore the best time of day for harvesting leaf plants such as the white cabbage pictured here.

In the afternoon, forces stream from above downwards. It is best to harvest root plants then, such as the onion.

Harvest times

Plant	Harvest time	Special conditions
Root plants for winter storage	Root days, preferably during descending moon	Not on leaf days
Fruit plants	Fruit days	During ascending moon for storing
Leaf plants	On flower or fruit days if intended for storage; likewise herbs or leaves for teas; and cabbage for making *sauerkraut* (pickled cabbage) etc.	Flower days for cabbage
Flower plants	On flower days	

If vegetables are picked for immediate use, they can be harvested at any time, irrespective of such conditions: the fresher the better!

Kitchen herbs for immediate use can likewise be harvested at any time

The best conditions for harvest also apply to preserving of all kinds: juices, jellies, marmalades, jams, pickling and drying.

The time of day

In the early part of the day, forces stream up from below - which is why lettuce harvested then stays fresh longer.

In the afternoon and evening they stream down into the roots from above, and that is the best time of day to harvest root-crops.

It is not a good idea to harvest at midday.

THE SOIL

The basis of our soil is rock that has been eroded by the elements of water, air, light and heat. Depending on the original type of rock, different kinds of soil arise with varying characteristics, such as calcareous soil. Eroded rock and stone forms the mineral or inorganic part of our garden soil - which needs to be complemented by organic substance in order to sustain plants and crops. Soil organisms 'break down' the soil's inorganic and organic components to form a new unity: living, fertile soil. The life forces which derive from organic material raise the inorganic, mineral part of the soil halfway towards the living realm of the plant. Thus we call rock the basis or foundation.

So rock forms the base substance of soil. Through its erosion 'clay' comes about. 'Life' comes from the plant,

Trials over many years with sunflowers (behind) and flax (in front) have continually shown the same thing: that sowing on fruit days yields the greatest amount of seeds.

and we preserve this life through composting. The compost then enlivens the 'clay'.

The animal kingdom has, besides life, an additional property, that of instinct and impulse. When an animal dies, this quality remains connected with the dead body and 'decomposes'. Composting, with the help of soil organisms, transforms this instinct and impulse into living processes. But if we fertilize directly with horn, bones, skin, hair, feathers, wool or bristles, without composting first, then this animal nature is absorbed by the plant in unmediated form and attracts animal pests.

The three factors, 'clay' (from rock), 'life' (from the plant) and 'feeling' (from the animal) enable soil worked on by human beings to take up cosmic forces. Gardeners and farmers, as we have already seen (pages **23** onwards), need to make use of the most favourable cosmic impulses in this process. Then we can grow plants which provide the best and healthiest nourishment.

Soil testing

We have found time and time again that soil analyses produce different results according to the constellation in which the sun stands at the time of testing. Different samples can therefore only be compared with one another when they are taken at the same time.

In the northern hemisphere the highest nitrogen content occurs when the sun is in Bull and Virgin; and in the southern hemisphere when it is in Goat.

The moon also influences nitrogen content via hoeing. Highest nitrogen levels can be measured when hoeing is carried out with the moon in Bull, Virgin and Goat.

Working the soil

Every time we work the soil, cosmic forces stream into it - which is why all hoeing should be carried out only at times favourable to a particular kind of plant. As we have seen, these favourable times are the same as sowing times: for example leaf plants like lettuce should be sown and hoed on leaf days.

We can also choose the time of hoeing to affect germination of weed seeds. (See the chapter on 'Weeds'.)

We have found that it is not a good idea to work the soil at midday.

Autumn

Once the last plants have been harvested, we can begin preparatory work for the following year. If there is enough time after the soil has been worked to a shallow depth, then it is a good idea to sow a green manure crop.

It is best to choose green manure plants which complement cultivated plants (see pages **58** onwards).

At least every three years we should leave our beds and plots bare over winter (fallow, or winter furrow). This allows the soil to take up winter's cosmic forces. 23 years of tests and trials on various soil cultivation methods, carried out at Giessen University under the supervision of Professor Boguslawski and Dr Debruck, showed that the best results were obtained by leaving ploughed soil bare over winter.

Our comparative tests have shown for decades that soil quality in spring is best after leaving ploughed soil bare (winter furrow) throughout the winter.

Nature also furnishes us with an example of the positive effect of open ground in winter. In warm winters when there is too high a moisture content in the soil of low-lying fields, the mole transforms them into a landscape of bumps and hillocks. The earth is thus exposed to winter's cosmic forces. Every farmer and gardener knows that mole-hill soil is rich and fertile, and is glad to use it for seedbeds or spreading on fields.

Spring

In spring, once the land has grown dryer, cultivation can begin: the soil is worked thoroughly in preparation for sowing.

If the plot was previously covered in weeds, it is a good idea to till it when

34

The soil from mole-hills is particularly fertile, because it has been exposed to winter's cosmic forces.

the moon is in Lion. This stimulates the weed seeds to germinate. For the next 10 to 14 days one leaves the soil alone and waits for a favourable sowing constellation (e.g. a root day for sowing root vegetables). When this arrives, one can work the earth once more, hoeing the weed seedlings under. Then the soil is ready for sowing. We have found that beds prepared in this way no longer suffer from excessive weeds (see drawing on page **36**).

We don't manure in spring, but in autumn, for we have found that the animal quality present in dung attracts illnesses and pests.

Depth of cultivation

Cosmic forces work most strongly into the soil when it is worked to a depth of at least 10cm before sowing.

But hoeing need only reach a depth of 3cm. This aerates the soil so that cosmic forces can penetrate it. Hoeing alters the relationship between nitrogen, calcium carbonate, potassium, phosphorus and manganese, as well as various trace elements. If we simply mulch all the time instead of hoeing, this does not happen.

Soil warmth

The moment when the element of warmth stirs in the soil is of decisive importance. As this warmth becomes active, certain processes begin in the mineral realm, and only then can plant growth receive the impetus it needs.

Depending on cosmic influences, this moment can arrive at any time between the end of March and the middle of May. We give it in our *Sowing and Planting Calendar* each year.

Cultivation in spring on soil heavily affected by weeds.
Left: When the moon is in Lion, the soil, once dry enough, is well cultivated. This constellation stimulates many weed seeds to germinate.
Middle: Then one leaves the soil alone for 10 to 14 days, waiting for a constellation favourable to the kind of plant to be sown. When this arrives, the soil is cultivated again, and the germinated weeds are hoed under.
Right: Now sowing or planting can take place: in this case, lettuce on a leaf day with the moon descending.

MULCHING

By mulching we mean covering the soil with organic (leaves or wilted grass cuttings) or inorganic material (plastic sheeting). Only organic mulching will be discussed here.

Covering the soil in this way has the advantage of suppressing weeds and protecting the soil in times of drought. However it also has important disadvantages.

The covering serves many pests - above all slugs and snails - as nursery and hideout. So it is good to be clear why you are mulching before you set about it.

We actually never mulch, considering that the disadvantages outweigh other considerations.

37

COMPOST

The compost boxes on our farm.

choose a shady place in the garden and hammer the tomato stakes into the ground in squares, at one-metre intervals. The battens are placed in pairs upon each other, their ends crossing inside the tomato stakes. The ground within each square is covered with a little old compost, which helps get the rotting process started. Organic refuse matter is then added daily in layers, and moistened.

In recent years, fortunately, it has been generally recognized that compost really is worth its weight in gold for the garden. Many different composting methods are practised. Some people think kitchen peelings and refuse should be pre-composted before being included in the heap, or that worms should be added to it, or that expensive compost containers should be used. For years we have been using a simple and cheap method that has proved very effective.

Taking four tomato stakes, and untreated battens 1.25 m long (battens 2.5 m long can be sawn in half), we

We have been making these kinds of compost heaps for many decades. On the ground inside the batten-boxes, which should be in a shady place, we put a little old compost first, then well-mixed organic refuse, and always cover the heap immediately. Now and then we scatter a handful of bone- or hornmeal or guano on the heap. As the heap grows, we raise the height of the boxes by adding more battens. The rotting process can be made quicker by pouring 'cowpat preparation' on the heap once a month (see later chapter). Once the heap is half a metre high, we add the compost preparations. It is very important to keep the heap moist at all times.

We always cover the heap with a straw or reed mat, or a piece of old carpet. Now and then one can scatter a handful of horn- or bonemeal or guano over it. But it is important to keep everything moist. Pouring cow-dung preparation over the heap once a month helps speed up the rotting process. Once the heap is half a metre high, biodynamic gardeners add the compost preparations. The amateur gardener can also order these and use them as directed (see appendix).

Tests have shown that the heap rots down better and fertility-loss is minimized when the heap is well-moistened, the compost preparations are inserted and the compost is covered with a thin layer of garden peat. We use compost made this way after half a year.

We advise against including certain materials in the compost heap: cooked kitchen refuse, and the peels of citrus fruits or bananas which have not been organically grown. The peels go mouldy and form antibiotics which interfere with the micro-organisms that aid rotting. But this does not happen if you put the peels in a sealed jar of water and let them ferment, and then add them to the compost.

Left above: Ink-cap mushrooms are the first stage of decomposition in a manure heap. They need light, and grow on the outside of the heap when it is moist enough.

Left below: The second fungus stage occurs in the inside of the compost pile - here in the form of small field mushrooms.

COMPOST

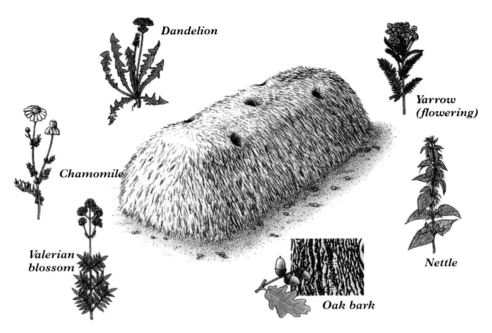

Dandelion

Yarrow
(flowering)

Chamomile

Valerian
blossom

Nettle

Oak bark

Once the compost heap is completed, various preparations are added to it, to encourage a balanced rotting process. These preparations, made from yarrow, chamomile, nettle, oak bark and dandelion, must be inserted as directed in small holes in the compost heap. The final preparation, made from valerian, is watered in liquid form over the whole heap.

Weeds which easily reproduce vegetatively (such as couch grass and bindweed), through root runners for example, feel very much at home in a compost heap. They reproduce to their hearts' content, and if you are not careful can be returned to growing beds along with the rotted compost. For that reason we first let them decompose in water, making a liquid manure of them, before adding them to the compost (see pages **75** onwards).

Time and again people tell us that adding compost to their soil increases the number of weeds. This only happens if composting is not done in the right way. If flowering weeds, or ones which have already produced seed, are put on the compost heap, one must just make sure that the seeds germinate before the compost is returned to the soil. By keeping the compost moist one can ensure that the seeds germinate. They will soon die again since conditions

41

in the heap are not conducive to their growth.

All available manures and organic refuse should be composted. When animal body substances (such as bristle, horn or bones) are used to fertilize the soil without prior composting, they encourage fungal and pest attack.

Finally I would like to emphasize the advantage of mature compost over fresh, uncomposted manure. 1000 kilogrammes of mature compost per hectare achieves the same effect as 4000 kilogrammes per hectare of fresh manure. In addition, numerous studies have shown that the rotting process makes organic substances fit for creating good soil structure and bringing about healthy plant growth.

Vegetarian compost

We carried out studies on composts which had no animal substances added to them, and came up with some astonishing results. On the positive side, plants nourished by such compost produced very healthy growth and did not suffer from pests. We even observed that pests on nearby beds, treated with other kinds of compost, stayed where

View of one of our trial fields. Spinach sown on leaf days (in front) grows best. Plants sown at perigee (middle) are small and lice-infested. Spinach sown on fruit days (behind the onions) has already started forming seeds.

Lettuce, for example, loses the capacity to produce a full 'head' when it is nourished for years only with compost to which no animal substances have been added.

they were and did not 'emigrate'. On the other hand, though, plants cultivated for several years with only vegetarian compost, increasingly lost their capacity to develop fully - failing for instance to produce a full 'head' of cauliflower or lettuce.

Weed compost

When large quantities of seeding weeds are available, we build an extra compost heap from them, taking care to ensure that it is kept moist. It is a good idea to add some mature compost as well, to help speed up the rotting process.

The warmth produced in the heap stimulates the seeds to germinate quickly, but these seedlings cannot develop fully, and so die and rot down to substances useful to the soil. However it is very important to turn the topmost layer of 10cm after about two weeks, since there is only enough light and oxygen for germination in this outer layer. After germination has occurred, we cover the heap with grass and cuttings etc. The heap must be kept moist. In dry weather one should water

it once a week. The compost should only be used when it has rotted right down to soil - after about a year.

Our analyses showed that weed compost contained a high nitrogen content, often considerably higher than compost made from other plant remains.

Compost from grass cuttings

Grass cuttings produce good compost soil. We build the heap with grass cuttings mixed with some earth, old compost or leaves, so that it does not become too acidic. It is best to let the grass wilt a little before adding it to the heap, which later helps it to break down more quickly. It is a good idea to add 1 kg quicklime to every 3 cubic metres of grass cuttings.

Quick composting of animal substances

When using animal substances such as bone– and hornmeal, bristles, wool, feathers or guano for making specialized composts (usually for seed-drills or planting holes), there is a special process which makes them rot down quickly. (However this process is not ideal - it is better to convert these substances properly within a compost heap.)

For quick rotting, mix 80% mature plant compost with 20% of the animal substance, and make small heaps. They must be well-moistened, then covered with straw, and finally watered once again. If there is no straw available, one could also use a tarpaulin or blanket if necessary. The first stage of decomposition is completed after about five or six weeks - you can tell this from a white coating which appears on the outer surface of the heap. At this point you can use the specialized compost, and plants nourished by it will be far less subject to attack by moulds and fungi than they would otherwise have been (see page **79**).

Quick composting of animal substances

We take 80% mature plant compost and 20% animal body substances. After mixing these well, small heaps are made, and moistened thoroughly. Finally they are covered with straw and watered once more. After five or six weeks a white coating appears on the heap (middle drawing). Now we can use the specialized compost.

THE NETTLE AND ITS USES

The stinging nettle (*Urtica dioica*) possesses many useful properties. It is used, after a special pre-composting process, as one of the bio-dynamic compost preparations.

The earth produced by nettle compost is very well suited to growing delicate plants, and for nourishing roses and strawberries. The only other compost with similar qualities is one made from well-rotted pine needles.

The nettle can also be used to counteract pests and encourage growth.

The following 'recipes' should be used to treat plants no more than three times. Further treatments can reduce their storage and germinating capacities. The same thing can happen if this liquid manure is made and used in stronger doses than recommended.

The stinging nettle (Urtica dioica) possesses many good properties which we can make use of in gardening.

24-hour brew

Cut 1 kg fresh nettles. They can be in flower but should not yet have formed seeds.

Place the nettles in a wooden, clay or enamel vessel and pour 10 litres of cold or lukewarm water on them. Leave standing for 24 hours, then pour through a sieve.

This extract helps against larval and caterpillar infestation, and should be applied three times within several hours. It is sprayed finely over plants.

We use stinging nettles against pests, and to stimulate growth, making a 24-hour extract or liquid manure from them. See text for recipe and use.

Stinging nettle as forcing manure ('nettle Jauche')

Place 1 kg fresh stinging nettle (they can have flowered, but not yet produced seeds) in an enamel container, to which is added 10 litres cold or lukewarm water. Leave until the leaves have rotted - which depends on external temperature. From eight

46

days to four weeks later, the liquid manure will be ready.

This is a powerful manure and should therefore only be used in dilution. Dilute 1 litre liquid manure with 9 litres of water for fine spraying on the soil; and for watering mix 1 litre liquid manure with 40 litres water.

Hold-ups in growth caused by cold weather, often followed by pest infestation, can be counteracted by watering or spraying with stinging nettle liquid. This should be done in the early morning or evening, followed by watering.

In trials we observed that treating roses, currant bushes and fruit trees on three consecutive evenings got rid of pests and often also moulds and fungi.

Stimulating growth with stinging nettle manure

This liquid manure is made as already described.

However the dilution is different: 0.25 litres liquid manure is mixed with 10 litres water, for watering such plants as tomatoes, cucumbers, spinach and cabbage. This should be done three times during the growing period.

If you wish to spray it, dilute 0.5 litres liquid manure with 10 litres water and stir for 15 minutes. Then spray with a very fine nozzle.

Potatoes are extremely grateful for this treatment, as well as currant bushes which we spray after harvest.

LIQUID MANURES FROM HERBS

Other plants besides nettles can be used to make liquid manures, such as thistle, milk thistle, comfrey and chickweed. Even herbs which we use in the kitchen can serve the same purpose. So if we have any artemisia, chamomile, lavender, yarrow or lemon balm left over, we can turn them into liquid manure (1 kg fresh herbs to 10 litres water). Then we can add 1 litre of the liquid to 40 litres water - no higher concentration than this - and water plants with it. Any liquid or plant remains left over can be added to the compost heap.

From comfrey (Symphytum officinale, left) and true chamomile (right) we can make liquid manures.

COWHORN MANURE AND COWHORN SILICA PREPARATIONS

Radishes from a rhythm and preparations trial, which showed a difference of roughly 40%.

The **cowhorn manure preparation** (preparation '500') and cowhorn silica preparation (silica preparation '501') are indispensable for biodynamic gardening.

The cowhorn manure preparation is made from cow manure. It helps establish a good relationship between plant and earth forces. If one sprays it at sowing then the plant can develop more roots, and thus supply the part of the plant above ground with more nourishment. We also use it when replanting. This is particularly important when we cannot, for some reason, plant at the right constellation.

On biodynamic farms cow horns are filled with cow manure in late September or early October. These are buried in the earth and remain there over winter. The horn 'sucks up' the forces present in the earth in winter, and unites them with the manure. In spring the horn is dug up and its contents are placed in an earthenware container. This is sealed with a lid and kept in loose peat until needed. Cowhorn manure can be used for up to two years.

49

For our agricultural fields we stir 30 g of cowhorn preparation into 10 litres of water. Get a good spiral motion going in the bucket or container, from the outside in. Only one person should stir (for precise instructions see page **51**). This will provide enough for spraying 2,500 square metres of soil. Gardeners need proportionally less, depending on their acreage. Cowhorn preparation is sprayed three times before sowing, at roughly 10 minute intervals.

The **cowhorn silica preparation** enhances the forces emanating from the cosmos and constellations, so it should be sprayed on the days best suited to each particular type of plant. In other words, leaf plants like lettuce should be sprayed on leaf days.

Our tests demonstrated different specific results in different cases. For example, we found storage quality of cabbage was increased by

a last silica spraying on flower days before harvesting. Carrot quality was increased by giving a final spraying with the moon in Ram or Scales shortly before harvesting. The table below is intended to clarify this.

To make cowhorn silica preparation we use clear quartz or rock crystal, as far as possible uncontaminated by other substances. The fact that this is used industrially to manufacture magnifying glasses is an indication of its properties: sunlight passing through a magnifying glass can ignite paper. In other words, the effect of light and heat is intensified, and this is the same property that we make use of in cultivation. We place finely powdered quartz in a cowhorn, whose spiral tendency, according to the spiritual scientific research of Rudolf Steiner, exerts a focusing and concentrating effect on biological processes. The horn is placed in the

Application of silica preparation

Plants	Time of silica spraying
Root plants	On root days: three times a month (in other words, on root days roughly every nine days), in the early morning after sunrise
Leaf plants	On leaf days: three times a month, in the early morning after sunrise
Flower plants	On flower days: three times a month, after sunrise
Fruit/seed plants	On fruit/seed days: three times a month, after sunrise

earth during the summer, and magnifies and concentrates the effect of summer sunlight in the silica preparation.

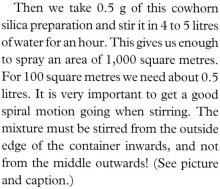

When stirring preparations, with a wooden or bamboo stick for instance, it is very important to get a good spiral motion going. We stir from outside inwards, which concentrates forces rather than dispersing them. Only one person should stir a mixture. Once a good spiral motion has been obtained, we remove the stick and allow it to 'reverberate' for a while. Then we stir again, but this time in the opposite direction.

Then we take 0.5 g of this cowhorn silica preparation and stir it in 4 to 5 litres of water for an hour. This gives us enough to spray an area of 1,000 square metres. For 100 square metres we need about 0.5 litres. It is very important to get a good spiral motion going when stirring. The mixture must be stirred from the outside edge of the container inwards, and not from the middle outwards! (See picture and caption.)

The spiral motion inwards 'sucks' in forces from outside. If one stirs from inside outwards, forces are dispersed instead of being concentrated. The preparation, once stirred, must be used within the next three to four hours, otherwise it loses its effect. It is very important to ensure that only one person does the stirring for each mixture.

We produce both preparations ourselves at our research station. The process is possibly too laborious for most amateur gardeners, who may also find it difficult to obtain the horns and manure, or find a suitable place for burying them. These preparations can be obtained from the address listed at the end of this book (but gardeners must still of course do their own stirring!)

Directions for making the 'spraying brew' accompany the preparations. (See also the instructions on page **54**.)

THE COWPAT PREPARATION

Unfortunately it is hard to get hold of the cowpat preparation if one cannot, or does not wish, to make it oneself. You can get further advice from the Biodynamic Association (address at the end of book).

Cow manure is the 'base substance', the medium which 'carries' the three main components of this preparation: eggshells, basalt and compost preparations. The manure should if possible come from cows on a biodynamic farm. It is a good idea to give them fodder with a high roughage content for a few days, so that the manure is well formed. The eggshells, too, should come from a biodynamic farm.

Five 10-litre buckets of pure cowdung, 100 g of dry, crushed eggshells, and 500 g basalt sand (grains between 0.2 and 0.5 mm) are placed in a wooden tub, then turned and stirred with a spade to activate the mixture.

The first half of it is put in an old wooden barrel without a bottom (!) that has been buried to a depth of about 40-50 cm in the ground outside. The earth dug out to make a hole for it is piled up against the outside of the barrel. To this first half we add a half portion of compost preparations (see section on compost), inserted individually as in a compost heap. Then we add the second half of the mixture, and insert the second portion of compost preparations, again individually.

Next we stir five drops of valerian preparation for ten minutes in a litre of water, pour this 'valerian water' over the contents of the barrel, then cover the barrel with a wooden lid or board.

The cowpat preparation: it has been treated as described, and is ready for use.

THE COWPAT PREPARATION

Making the cowpat preparation

Five 10-litre buckets of cow dung, 100 g finely crushed eggshells and 500 g basalt sand (grains from 0.2 to 0.5 mm) are stirred and turned in a wooden vat for an hour. Then we place the mixture and the compost preparations (see text) in a wooden barrel without a bottom sunk in the ground, and leave it for four weeks. Then we turn it with a spade once more. After a further four weeks we can start to use it.

We leave the barrel for four weeks, then briefly stir the contents with a spade again. After a further four weeks the cowpat preparation can be used.

For our farming trials we stir 60 g cowpat preparation in 10 litres of water for an hour (getting a good, inward turning spiral motion going, as described earlier). This amount is sufficient for spraying 2,500 square metres. Gardeners will need correspondingly less water and preparation.

We obtained the best results by spraying three times on consecutive days (three to five days before sowing). One stirring can be used over two or three days, and is sprayed towards evening.

The cowpat preparation activates soil and soil organisms, encouraging better soil structure and quicker breakdown of inorganic and organic substances. We also recommend spraying it when a green manure is ploughed in, or when manure or compost is applied (once in each case). We also spray it on winter furrows (once).

The cowpat preparation is used in all countries where biodynamic farming and gardening are practised. We are not yet in a position to say whether the 'base substance' could be made equally well from the dung of other animals, such as sheep, goats, horses, chickens or rabbits. We are currently experimenting on this in numerous trials, and will be able to release our results in a few years' time.

Note: cowhorn manure, cowhorn silica and cowpat preparations must be strained through a sieve before spraying. The sieve must have a very fine mesh - something like a hair-sieve. A double layer of nylon stocking is still better. This stops the spray nozzle from getting blocked.

ROCK MEAL

Powdered or ground stone can be used for fertilizing plants, but it is still necessary to compost it first. It can be added in small quantities to the compost and improves its quality, since it stimulates clay formation in the soil.

Basalt meal

This is particularly useful. Basalt is a relatively young rock, which has passed through a fire process but has not been metamorphosed through combustion. We regard basalt meal as a soil 'medicine', which is why it should be added to the soil only in small quantities and via the composting process. Such medicines do not work when used in the same quantities as fertilizer.

Berry harvest

GREEN MANURING

Green manuring refers to the growing of a green crop containing specific kinds of plants - the green manure plants. These plants remain in the soil either for a shorter period (a few weeks) or a longer one (over winter), and are then usually cut while still green and dug into the soil. Sometimes they are also used as cattle fodder.

There are many advantages of green manuring. It protects the soil and provides a change of crop. Certain green manure crops, such as the leguminous plants, are able to take in nitrogen from the atmosphere and transfer it to the soil. By hoeing these plants under we provide the earth with organic materials and stimulate the life of the soil.

Soil analyses have shown a higher phosphorus content after cultivation of cornflower, phacelia and corn campion. Phacelia and corn campion also increased the potassium content, while a higher calcium carbonate content was obtained after peas and lupins had been grown.

The sowing time for a green manure crop depends on the way in which one wishes to use it. If you want plentiful leaf growth for cattle fodder, it should be sown on a leaf day. The leguminosae, whose root-nodules concentrate nitrogen, should be sown on root days.

The green manure should be cut and worked into the soil when the moon is descending (planting time). This helps forces to work downwards into the earth, which aids decomposition processes in the soil. We also recommend spraying

The lupin is an excellent green manure plant.

the cowpat preparation to speed up these processes.

Recommended green manure plants for the garden are: berseem clover, lupins, phacelia, vetchling or meadow pea, and rye.

The green manure plant phacelia. Phacelia is both attractive to bees and good for the soil.

The green manure crop (here rye) should be worked into the soil when the moon is descending (planting time). The rye shown here is for digging under in the autumn. In spring it would be turned under when the plants are smaller.

CROP CHANGE AND ROTATION

Crop change refers to planting different types of crop on the same piece of soil. It is important not to replant a crop of the *same family* in the same soil for several years. We thus avoid crop illnesses and prevent the soil exhausting itself of specific nutrients, and accumulating too many of the same waste products. Cabbage, for instance, should not be planted after cauliflower.

When too much is demanded of soils, by planting the same or related types of plant after too short an interval or after none, the first signs are poor growth, followed by illnesses and pests. We can keep the plants alive with

In planning crop rotation one should remember to include green manure plants in the cycle. Mustard, for instance, belongs to the cruciferous plants, of which the cabbages are a member.

The plant has a fivefold existence - root/leaf/blossom/fruit/seed. In practice however, we recognize a fourfold division into root, leaf, blossom and fruit/seed.

This can become clear if we look at a specific plant family - the cruciferae for instance: radishes concentrate their forces in the root (above left). The cabbages, such as red cabbage (below left) hold back the 'stem' forces, which strive upwards, in their leaves and 'head'. The cauliflower (above right) goes a stage further and burgeons into a flower-like creation. Since there are no cruciferae which we sow for their seeds in the garden, a closely related weed, shepherd's purse, can 'fill the gap'. Rape (below right) is grown agriculturally for its oil.

pesticides, but long-term, irremediable damage is done to crop quality. Yet proper crop rotation can avoid this arising in the first place.

The amateur gardener often finds crop rotation a problem because of lack of space, and because the same types of vegetable are always in demand. At the beginning of the year we should draw up a good rotation plan, and write down what we plant through the year. Otherwise it is easy to lose sight of what has actually been planted.

Many books recommend a rotational cycle of: heavy feeders - light feeders - leguminosae. But we have found that this soon leads to a situation in which pesticides become necessary. The plants grew sick, had to be treated and were poor in quality.

The most effective rotational cycle takes account of *plant families*. The plant disease club root can help demonstrate this. This is a growth which affects cabbage (and cruciferae) roots, caused by a fungus living in the soil. Not

only white cabbage and kohlrabi are affected, but also rape, radishes etc. - which all belong to the same family. Green manure crops such as mustard are also affected. In such cases a different green manure crop should be chosen - phacelia for instance. We recommend that five years should pass before the same type or family of plant is replanted in the same soil.

We must also consider the main part or 'organ' of the plant to be harvested when we are planning rotational cycles. The plant's five-fold existence which

An example of crop rotation which we have found effective: First year - cauliflower (above far left). Second year - beetroot (below far left). Third year - dwarf beans (above left). Fourth year - potatoes (below left). Then strawberries for the next few years (right).

it strives to fulfil: root-leaf-blossom-fruit/seed, relates back to the cosmic influences described at the beginning of this book, which correspond exactly with these five 'stages'. A crop rotation must take them into account.

In the cruciferae family, for instance, to which the cabbages belong, radishes concentrate growth forces in their swelling roots. The cabbages themselves, meanwhile, hold back the upward-striving 'stem' forces in their leaves, wrapping one leaf around another to produce a full head. The kohlrabi thickens and swells in its stem region; and the cauliflower presents us with its delectable, flower-like 'heart'. There are no species of cruciferae that are sown in the garden for their seed. Rape is grown agriculturally for its seed. Garden weeds of this family - such as sheherd's purse and pennycress - can fill this 'gap', so that the full range of relationship with the soil comes about.

Not only a different plant family, therefore, but also a different plant 'organ' should be grown in a subsequent year. For practical purposes we see the five-fold division described above in terms of four: root, leaf, blossom and fruit/seed.

So we recommend that a plot where leaf plants are cultivated in the first year should be planted with a root crop in the second. In the third year plants should be chosen in which the forces held back in lower regions (root) can be raised up to the plant's upper sphere (seed or fruit). Just as we ourselves need to breathe out fully before inhaling again, so must the soil too - and this is what the third year allows. In the fourth year we should plant blossom plants. These will not be tempted to shoot into seed since any excess seed forces in the soil will have been used up the previous year.

By taking account of both plant family and plant organ in this way, the best possible conditions are created both for the soil and for plant growth.

In the following examples of rotation, we will start from an old strawberry bed, one which is therefore due to be moved elsewhere. After the final strawberry harvest, the plants are chopped back and their green parts are put on the compost heap. Then the bed is dug over and rye grass with lupins is sown. We have found it very beneficial to let the soil have a grass cover now and then, and rye puts down deep roots, thus loosening the lower soil levels. The lupin, a leguminous plant, collects nitrogen and thus increases the amount of soil nutrients. In the spring these plants are then cut as a green manure and hoed under. This is a good starting point for planting cruciferae, such as cabbages.

The examples of rotation given below are only intended as a stimulus for each gardener to develop his or her own cycle, suited to particular conditions and circumstances. We have had very good results from this type of rotation. Our plants stayed healthy and produced high yields.

Strawberries can remain on the same bed for between five and eight years, after which the sequence begins again.

A few tips

– Instead of potatoes one can also plant flowers for cutting
– When growing potatoes you can sow lupins with them. There is no need to

bother about them much when hoeing. When the lupin flower buds start appearing, nip these off to encourage side shoots with increased leaf growth. This encourages more root pods to form, which gather nitrogen.
– Once tomatoes and cucumbers have been harvested in the autumn, vetch or sweet peas can be planted.

A few examples can show the reasons for the rotational cycles in the table above. Green cabbage needs to produce a loose and open leaf/stem structure. In the following year, therefore, onions can form without

Rotational cycle beginning with:

rye/lupin green manure after digging up old strawberry bed

year 1	year 2	year 3	year 4	year 5
White cabbage	Carrots	Peas	Potatoes	Strawberries
Red cabbage	Parsnips	Broad bean	Potatoes	Strawberries
Savoy cabbage	Black salsify or Scorzonera	Mange-tout peas	Potatoes	Strawberries
Curly kale	Onions	Sweetcorn	Potatoes	Strawberries
Brussel sprouts	Celeriac	Runner beans	Jerusalem artichoke	Strawberries
Kohlrabi	Leeks	Peppers	Jerusalem artichoke	Strawberries
Swedes	Chards	Cucumbers	Jerusalem artichoke	Strawberries
Small radishes	Parsley	Tomatoes	Jerusalem artichoke	Strawberries
Large radishes	Herbs	Cucumbers	Cutting flowers	Strawberries

hindrance from upward-striving 'stem' forces, which have already been used up.

Kohlrabi concentrates available forces on swelling its stem region, and is therefore ideal as a preparation for leeks, since too powerful stem forces would disturb the leaf-wrapping process, in which layer upon layer is packed closely together.

This kind of remark could be continued for pages and pages. But their real aim is to stimulate everyone to think for themselves and make their own observations.

Now there are also of course plants which have not been included in the table and which do not require a whole season before harvesting, such as spinach, lettuce, lamb's lettuce and endive. We treat these plants in the following way:

–Lettuce is sown as a 'marking seed' between carrots. (This is because carrots need a long time to germinate, while lettuce germinates quickly. This allows you to see where the seed-rows are when hoeing.) The young lettuce plants are later moved to the cabbage beds once they start to offer the carrots too much competition. By the time the cabbages have grown too large, the lettuce has long since been harvested - so they can grow side by side.

– Spinach and lamb's lettuce are sown at the edge of cucumber beds. They cover and protect the soil and are harvested before the cucumbers have grown big enough to need the space.

– Lettuce and spinach can be cultivated in spring as an early crop on beds which are later planted with a main crop.

– Lettuce, spinach and endive can be planted on beds where early cabbage, dwarf beans and early potatoes have been harvested

We have not yet found any negative rotational effects from planting 'in-between' crops in this way.

However, one must take particular care with the cruciferae. Short-lived plants like radish or garden cress should only be planted on cabbage beds. They can be sown at the edge. They must never be planted on beds where other plant families are growing, since this would disturb the five-year interval.

64

Kohlrabi (right) is the ideal preparatory crop for leeks (below). Kohlrabi concentrates forces in its thickened, swollen 'stem-fruit'. Leeks can then grow undisturbed by 'stem' forces that the kohlrabi have used up, and so can form dense, closely-packed tubes of leaves.

WATERING

You may well be surprised to hear that we don't water our crops, except for once after planting out, and when sowing grass - because the seed lies on the surface - and of course in the greenhouse. Even in drought years we produce good yields by observing a few basic laws of nature.

During the morning the soil breathes out, then breathes in again in the afternoon. Before noon the earth's forces stream upwards into the upper portions of the plant. In the afternoon and evening these forces descend and concentrate in the plant's lower parts, and stream on into the soil. One can make use of this fact.

If you want to increase the moisture in the soil, you can hoe in the evening, and the earth then breathes in moisture from its surroundings. If the earth is too wet, you can hoe in the morning to help it exhale its excess moisture.

We never water our plots except for once after re-planting and when sowing grass-seed. That does not apply, of course, to the greenhouse, where we have to water as much as necessary - in summer up to twice a day.

Only the top 3 cm are hoed, creating a loose layer that functions as a moisture regulator.

During the morning the earth breathes out (left), during the afternoon it breathes in (right)

When plants are accustomed to being watered their roots delve less deeply into the soil, so in hot, dry periods they become dependent on watering to survive. We have harvested carrots and parsnips whose tap roots were as long as 1.20 m, and 80 cm in onions. We have also found that repeated watering destroys soil structure - it becomes hard, and develops fissures in dry weather.

During dry periods one can mulch the beds. But this should be removed once rain has fallen again, otherwise it provides an ideal nest and breeding ground for slugs and snails.

In periods of drought we hoe towards evening on leaf and root days.

Night moisture and dew is also encouraged by spraying paths and grass towards evening with the cowhorn dung preparation (see pages 49 onwards) or the cowpat preparation (see pages 52 onwards).

Water quality

The sort of water one uses is of course important. We have learned from the water researcher Theodor Schwenk[4] that our water quality can be improved by allowing streams and rivers to follow their own, natural movement and course. These researches led the

English sculptor John Wilkes to create 'flow-form' basins in which water can do just that.[5]

We carried out the following trial. Between our two ponds, one of which is higher up than the other, we placed 36 of these flowform basins; then, for a week, we watered seedlings in our greenhouse with the water that had passed through them. After planting out, these vegetables were treated like all the others - not watered in other words. Yet they showed significantly better growth. This type of 'dynamised' water, however, is not suitable for mixing preparations.

There are still many unanswered questions about water quality, which will need many further trials to resolve - not least in respect to the water we give our animals or drink ourselves. Many such researches are being conducted in various private or government-funded institutes, but there are as yet no definitive results or recommendations.

Water is stimulated into vortex movement when it flows through these forms, and subsequently enhances plant growth. Such basins were developed to regenerate sewage water.

LATE FROST IN MAY

A late frost in May can have debilitating effects on crops. We protect delicate plants with some kind of covering, such as a polytunnel or a cloche. If the frost still does its damage, we spray valerian water in the morning: this is made by adding one drop of valerian blossom juice (see appendix) to 1 litre of water, then stirring for 15 minutes. This mixture is sprayed on frost-damaged plants; and followed by a good watering one hour after spraying.

Extract of valerian flowers is diluted and sprayed on damaged plants in the morning after a late frost.

69

GOOD FRIDAY, EASTER SATURDAY

We have long noticed - for the past thirty years - that Good Friday and Easter Saturday are unsuited to sowing and planting out. Seedlings germinate poorly, and plants moved and replanted grow weak and often die altogether. These negative influences begin early on Good Friday and end before dawn on Easter Sunday.

Why? The events at Golgotha which took place 2,000 years ago still affect the earth each year. The plant-world is sensitive to this.

Left: kohlrabi, a leaf plant
Below: ruby chard, also a leaf plant.

WEEDS

Weeds can be an enormous problem, especially in agricultural-scale cultivation. But there are one or two basic rules which can make life much easier.

One trial we did on weed-growth produced astonishing results. We divided a field into several smaller areas, and for the next four weeks worked on a new area every second day. An initial soil-analysis had shown that all the soil within the field was the same. We found that the time at which we worked on a piece of land determined the kinds of weed which subsequently germinated there. In the first plot there was one main type of weed and very few others. On the second plot, which had been prepared for sowing two days later, the main type of weed was a quite different one.

We therefore came to the conclusion that neither the soil nor the plants grown could be responsible, but the time when the soil was cultivated - and therefore the cosmic influences at work. Further tests followed and showed us the best way of combating weeds.

When the moon is in Lion, all weeds germinate very well. So we recommend choosing this time to loosen the soil in the spring, before preparing seed-beds. The weeds germinate and can then be worked under into the soil after 10-14 days, after which sowing can take place. In this way the weeds actually contribute to the soil's health (see pages 35 and 36).

If the moon is in Goat during soil cultivation, very few weeds germinate, so it is a good idea to use this time for a final working and hoeing of the soil for potatoes and root crops.

We also had good results from spraying an 8x dilution made with seed ash, or by simply spreading weed-seed ash on the soil. Significantly fewer weeds grew on the beds after this treatment.

8x dilution for combating weeds

To make the 8x dilution, we burn many different kinds of weed seeds, on wood and preferably in a stove, when the moon is in Lion. A wood-burning charcoal grill can equally be used (see picture), and a small oven can be built on it with bricks, over which a metal sheet is placed.

WEEDS

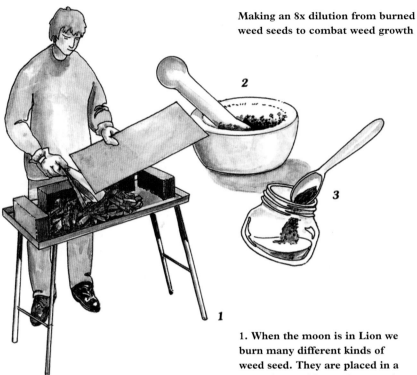

Making an 8x dilution from burned weed seeds to combat weed growth

2

3

1

1. When the moon is in Lion we burn many different kinds of weed seed. They are placed in a paper bag and burned on wood.
2. The ash from the burned weed seeds and the wood is ground with a pestle and mortar for an hour (by one person only).
3. From this 'dynamised' ash is produced an 8x dilution (see text).

It is best to place the seeds in a paper bag and put them into the wood-fire, which needs to be glowing red-hot. The seeds only burn properly in a red-hot glowing fire. We place a metal sheet over the bricks since the seeds otherwise spray all over the place like popcorn. Once the seeds have been completely burned and the ash has cooled, it is ground by one person for an hour in a pestle and mortar - 'dynamised' or made dynamic in other words. With root weeds, a little of the root should also always be burned. **It is important to see that the ash is a whitish-grey. If it is black the seeds have not yet burned enough.**

72

8x DILUTION FOR COMBATING WEEDS

Time of burning and spreading of weed-ash for combating weeds, if no homoeopathic potencies are made

Moon in	Plant to be burned
Fishes	Tufted vetch *(Vicia cracca)*
Ram	Wild mustard *(Sinapsis arvensis)*
	Charlock *(Raphanus raphanistrum)*
	Red dead-nettle *(Lamium purpureum)*
Bull	Ground elder *(Aegopodium podagraria)*
	Chervil *(Chaerophyllum hirsutum)*
	Goose grass *(Galium aparine)*
Twins	Wild oats *(Avena fatua)* and grasses
	Chickweed *(Stellaria media)*
	Corn grass *(Apera spica-venti)*
Crab	Buttercup *(Ranunculus)* and creepers
Lion	Dock *(Rumex)*
Virgin	Thistle *(Cirsium arvense)*
	Coltsfoot *(Tussilago farfara)*
	Horsetail *(Equisetum arvense)*
	Bindweed *(Convolvulus arvensis)*
Scales	Galinsoga *(Galinsoga parviflora)*
	Milk thistle
Scorpion	Black nightshade *(Solanum nigrum)*
Archer	Orach *(Atriplex)*
	Couch grass *(Agropyron repens)*
Goat	(very few weeds germinate at this time)
Waterman	Penny cress *(Thlaspi arvense)*
	Shepherd's purse *(Capsella bursa-pastoris)*
	Knot-grass *(Polygonum)*

Using seeds that have not been thoroughly combusted produces no effect at all. Once the ash is ready, the 8x dilution can be made: 1g of the dynamised ash mixture is placed in a small bottle together with 9ml of water and shaken for three minutes. This is now a 1x dilution. Then one adds 90ml of water and shakes for another three minutes: a 2x dilution. For the 3x

Chickweed (Stellaria media).

Then we add 90ml water again, shake for a further three minutes, then add to this 6x dilution 900ml water and shake to produce 7x. Finally we add 9 litres of water to the 7x, shake or stir for another three minutes - and have arrived at an 8x dilution.

Of this 8x, one needs about 0.5 litres for 100 square metres of soil area. Spraying should be done three times, at intervals of a few hours.

Many people also effectively combat weeds with seed-ash that has not been dynamised and potentised. To do this it is important that we take account of the moon-rhythms of individual plants, if only one particular weed-type is to be dealt with (see table on previous page). In this case we just burn seeds of this one type of weed. Otherwise we gather a mixture of weed-seeds and burn them with the moon in Lion, and then strew the ash on the surfaces where weeds are causing problems. As Rudolf Steiner describes it, one does this in a similar way to adding pepper to a meal - and once only, when the soil is being cultivated for sowing.

dilution a further 900ml water must be added; for 4x a further 9 litres of water.

After each addition of water the mixture is shaken again for three minutes. Between 3x and 4x one can also stir it for three minutes.

Since, if one carried on in this way, an 8x dilution would result in 100,000 litres of water, it is better to proceed with a smaller quantity from the 4x dilution onwards. To do this, we take 1ml of the 4x mixture and add 9ml water, and after shaking for three minutes we have a 5x dilution.

Prevention

We have often observed that un-composted animal substances, such as horn, bone, bristle, feathers, wool, blood, or bonemeal encourage weed-growth. It is therefore very important to compost them first if one wants to use them for improving soil quality or fertilizing.

Liquid manure from weeds ('Jauche')

Liquid manure made from weeds can be used to get rid of the very weeds it contains. We have had good results from liquid manure made from creeping and climbing weeds, which anyway should not be put on the compost heap (see pages **40** onwards).

Recipe

We take the shoots and root parts of, for example, thistle, goutweed (herb Gerard), buttercup, coltsfoot, mint varieties and couch grass, as well as the whole plant of chickweed. and place them in a water-butt with water. On leaf-days we stir the contents around a little.

Making liquid manure from weeds

1. The shoots, tendrils and root-parts of the weeds are placed in a water-butt with water. On leaf days this mixture is stirred a little.
2. Once the plants have completely rotted down, the sieved liquid manure is sprayed, with the moon in Crab, wherever the weeds are not wanted. You can find in the text how, and how often to do this.

Once the plants have completely rotted down, the liquid is sieved and sprayed when the moon is in Crab. Wherever these weeds grow can be sprayed on three consecutive evenings, and this can cause them to disappear entirely.

The liquid manure can also be used to encourage the growth of cabbages, cucumbers and tomatoes - but only in a well-diluted form (1 litre to 10 litres water).

It can also be used to improve compost quality. Compost treated with it shows good growing properties.

We have already seen elsewhere (page **43**) that whole compost heaps can be made from weeds.

Various weeds

In what follows we would like to look at a few particular weeds, which we have found out certain things about in the course of our research.

Field thistle

The field thistle *(Cirsium arvense)* often appears where the soil is or has been strongly compacted.

One can mow the thistles when the moon is in Aquarius or Sagittarius, which releases a strong flow of sap. If one takes care to keep mowing them whenever the moon is ascending, the roots can no longer be sufficiently nourished by the leaves and the plants die.

Rumex autosa (dock)

This variety of dock has taken hold on our soil because of acid rain. It can be combated by continual cutting with the moon in Archer or Waterman. It can also be prevented from propagating itself via its seeds by making a seed-ash or 8x dilution and using it when the sun and moon are in Lion.

Horsetail, bindweed and coltsfoot

These three root-weeds, horsetail *(Equisetum arvense)*, bindweed *(Convolvulus arvensis)* and coltsfoot *(Tussilago farfara)* appear on soils which have high levels of underground water. The first step in combating them is to put in a drainage system to take away the water. If the water collects in impermeable layers of clay, compost should be added to the soil, which reduces the number of weeds.

VARIOUS WEEDS

Horsetail is a root-weed which we are not at all glad to see in our garden. However its positive qualities can be made very good use of in protecting other plants (see next chapter).

Coltsfoot (Tussilago farfara)

FUNGAL PLANT DISEASES

In nature, fungus has the general function of breaking down things which are dying. When we find stump fungi or honey agaric on old tree-stumps in summer, for instance, we know that a natural rotting process has begun. Field mushrooms which grow where horse or cow-dung has fallen, transform the substances present there.

Fungus belongs in the uppermost layer of the soil, where it can fulfil its tasks. So why does it sometimes leave its natural dwelling place and take up lodging on plants? Why does it settle on seeds and damage them, inducing people to coat them with poison (seed-dressing)? Is it because dying-processes are at work here too?

Rudolf Steiner tells us in his 'Agricultural Course' that fungi leave their natural abode, the surface of the soil, when moon forces start to work too strongly in the earth. Moon forces

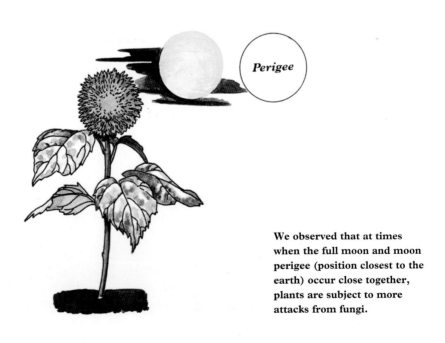

Perigee

We observed that at times when the full moon and moon perigee (position closest to the earth) occur close together, plants are subject to more attacks from fungi.

78

work through the watery element and can become too pervasive after heavy rainfall. By treating the soil with 'tea' made from horsetail *(Equisetum arvense)* the fungi can be made to return to soil level. This tea must be sprayed on the soil on which affected plants are growing.

We have long observed that moon forces become too strong in the soil in years of extremely high precipitation. They also become very powerful when full-moon and perigee (when the moon is closest to the earth) fall close together. In both cases this results in increased fungal attack on cultivated plants. We use horsetail tea as a preventative treatment at these times.

Our many years of observations have established that there are three main reasons for increased fungal attack. By following the advice below you are not likely to need any additional means of combating it:

1. Moon-forces are too strong, for instance in years of very high precipitation. Hoeing in the morning helps, since this enables the soil to exhale excess moisture.
2. Bad manuring, for instance with unrotted organic manure or un-composted animal body substances. The best preventative measure against fungal attack is to spread well-rotted compost in the autumn.
3. Seeds which were harvested during

The horsetail, Equisetum arvense, is capable of getting fungi which have 'crept up' plants to return to soil-level.

unfavourable constellations grow in the following year into plants which are susceptible to fungal attack.

The horsetail

The horsetail *(Equisetum arvense)* is able to make fungi growing on plants return to their natural level, that of the soil. How can it do this?

Let us look firstly at the marsh horsetail. The green plant develops first, then come the dark tips or caps harbouring the spores, by means of which the horsetail reproduces. Fungi also reproduce in this way.

The field or common horsetail on the other hand puts out a small stalk with brownish tips in early spring, from which spores are released to reproduce. Only later in the year does the green plant itself grow, without spore-tips, but with a high silica content. At this stage it has overcome the fungal level, and therefore has the capacity to return fungi to their proper place.

Anti-fungal recipes

Add 10 g of dried horsetail to 2 litres cold water and bring to the boil, boiling for 20 minutes in all. Then let the tea cool down. Now add a further 8 litres water and stir well for 10 minutes. The tea is then strained and can be sprayed in the evening (10 litres to 100 square metres), either under affected plants or as a preventative treatment. If trees show

Fighting fungal diseases: We make a tea from horsetail (see instructions in text). This is stirred well for ten minutes. Then we strain it and spray it in the evening under affected plants.

fungal growth, the trunks and thicker branches must also be sprayed.

In cases of severe and prolonged attack, this treatment can be repeated on three consecutive evenings.

Fungal diseases of various plants

The following are more specific observations and tips for particular vegetables and fruit.

Potatoes

Club-root is one of the most feared cabbage diseases.

These should not be hoed or earthed up on leaf days. The same applies to days when the moon is in perigee (closest to the earth). Otherwise they become susceptible to attack by the dreaded tuber- and haulm-rot fungus (blight).

Cabbage

The most feared fungal disease in cabbages is club-root, which is caused by the *Plasmodiosphora brassicae* fungus. The most important thing is to adhere carefully to a five-year crop rotation (see page **61**). Other cruciferous plants such as rape, shepherd's purse or green manure mustard can also be attacked, so this must be remembered when drawing up a rotation plan. It is also important to check that the soil has the right calcium balance. If the pH value is too low, fungal disease can spread more easily.

Strawberries

Garden strawberries need our particular attention. They grow low down near the natural fungus level, close to the surface of the soil. They are also usually fed with large quantities of manure, which brings about a strong watery tendency in them - though by nature they are at home in a warm, stony soil (as one can see in wild strawberries, which grow

81

Strawberries need our particular attention.

choosing either a flower or fruit day. The fruits should only be picked once morning dew has evaporated. Please also see the suggestions on pages **114** onwards.

Fruit trees

When choosing, planting and caring for fruit trees, thinking back for a moment to what our grandparents did can tell us whether we are on the right tracks.

Nowadays only short-stemmed fruit-trees are thought to be worth bothering with. Their 'crowns' have thus been brought down much closer to soil-level, to the fungal zone in other words. Tall or taller fruit-trees, however, are often healthier than shorter ones.

In former times great care was taken of the trunks of fruit-trees. In the 1820 edition of a 'D.I.Y.' book,[6] for instance, one can read about making a kind of thin gruel from cow-dung, lime, wood-ash and cow-hair. This was mixed with whey and stirred, and then painted on to fruit-tree trunks. (The cow-hair was obtained as a matter of course when cattle were brushed down twice daily. In those days it was unthinkable to let cows run about covered in their own dung, as they do now.)

Nowadays people feed trees with uncomposted manure, either to an area of soil corresponding to the crown ('crown-eaves') or even directly round

very healthily on rocky slopes). High levels of manuring encourage fungus.

So what can we do to help them?

The first thing is to make sure that we spread only well-rotted compost around them. In addition we should only plant and hoe them on fruit days. The time of harvest is also of great importance, and we recommend the trunk. This means that fungus has to become active there to break down the manure. Because of this, fungi are drawn up beyond their natural level and can attack wood, leaves and fruit.

Young fruit-trees should be cultivated and treated at times of favourable cosmic influence.

If these measures for preventing fungal disease are not sufficient, it is also possible to make up a liquid spraying manure from affected leaves.

Fungus-combating recipe for fruit-trees

Pick a few fungus-affected leaves and place them in a container of water (a handful of leaves to a 10-litre bucket of water). Let the leaves rot down completely. Then strain the mixture. When the moon is in Crab, spray it finely on trunks and crown. The soil under the tree should also be treated. Repeat the whole process twice more at intervals of four weeks.

For scab and mildew there is a further recommended treatment. Gather a handful of affected fruits lying beneath a tree, remove all the seeds from them (important!) and burn them on a wood-fire when the moon is in Scorpion. From the ash thus produced, an 8x dilution is made up. You can find the precise directions for doing this on page **91**. We spray the trunks, crowns and soil with this mixture on three consecutive days, then repeat the whole process again after four weeks.

ANIMAL PESTS

We call those animals 'pests' which want too much of a share in our vegetables and fruit. This is of course a rather subjective point of view. Mice, for instance, are pests to us because they like eating grain just as much as we do. A cat, however, has a rather different perspective on the matter! It is so fond of this animal that it first has a wonderful time playing around with it, then eats it up.

Again, greenfly are very unwelcome on our cultivated plants, but ants keep herds of them as milking 'cows', care for them and defend them from enemies, so as to drink the sweet excretions they produce.

In cases of insect attack, it often helps to water under affected plants in the evening with stinging nettle tea or highly diluted liquid manure made from nettles (see page **45**). Stinging nettles have a regulating effect on plant saps, which induces pests to leave them be. We have also noticed that warm rainfall has the same effect.

Besides cosmic rhythms, the amount of food available is of course also a significant factor affecting the numbers of animal pests. Buzzards lay more eggs in years when there are summer mice-plagues than in other years. Wild boar have larger numbers of offspring when oaks produce an abundance of acorns.

On the other hand some animals regulate themselves after a too copious reproduction which would threaten their own survival. Lemmings, for example, sometimes head for the sea in thousands to drown themselves.

When we think about how to best

The mouse is a pest for us, but not for the cat who likes eating it.

combat animal pests, we should remember that they only become pests by virtue of their excess numbers. In an ideally tended garden, such excess is very unlikely. If pests do appear in too numerous quantities, we need to look for the cause. Becoming familiar with the habits and life-cycles of such animals can be an important first step in affecting what is happening, and preventing extreme levels of plant damage. We have tried to pay heed to these aspects in the following list of plant-types.

Cabbage White caterpillars can do a great deal of damage to our cabbage plants.

Cabbage and carrot pests

Cabbage plants are susceptible to three main pests: the cabbage white butterfly, the turnip gall weevil and cabbage root fly. Carrots are mainly attacked by carrot fly.

Cabbage white

Every gardener knows these well: we see them as pretty butterflies fluttering about the garden in summer. In pest proportions we can deal with them by treating plants with wormwood tea or a 24-hour extract of stinging nettle.

Planting a few tomatoes between our cabbages sends the cabbage white on its way. Or one can lay side shoots removed from tomato plants between the cabbages.

The 24-hour stinging nettle extract is made as described on pages **45** onwards. The strained, undiluted liquid is sprayed finely on affected plants three times on the same day.

Turnip gall weevil

It is quite simple to drive this pest away. In May it searches for places to lay its eggs where cabbages are too closely planted, avoiding other beds. Another means of keeping it away is to cover seed-beds with a vegetable fly net (obtainable from specialist garden stores) on days in May when sun and moon are in Bull. Then it will pay a visit to your neighbour instead!

Cabbage root fly

The cabbage root fly appears in our gardens in April and May, when sun and moon are in Ram, and searches for suitable places to lay its eggs. The hatching maggots devour the skin of the root-collar and root.

Young cabbage plants should not be planted deeper in the earth than they previously grew in seed-beds. Nor should any earth be piled up around them. Doing either of these encourages the cabbage root fly.

Once affected, they can be treated as follows: apply a tea-spoon of undiluted wormwood tea (brewed in the same way as ordinary tea) directly to the collar of each root, repeating this three times within a few hours.

Carrot fly

As long as we make sure that we cultivate and tend carrots in the way they need, we can be almost certain that they won't be affected by carrot fly. Carrots like mature soils that have not been manured for two years. In

Above: turnip gall weevil in a 'gall' in a cabbage stem

Below: One can make a tea from wormwood and pour it directly on to the collar of the affected cabbage root. This helps get rid of cabbage root fly maggots.

Right: There's no need to fear the carrot fly if we give carrots what they need.

Below right: If the root-collar of the carrot is not covered over with earth, it turns green. The carrot becomes bitter, which cutworms find extremely tasty.

such conditions the plants can better develop their protein and form a high sugar content.

While late manuring detracts from the taste of carrots as far as we are concerned, it makes them more attractive for the carrot fly. It finds carrots cultivated like this ideal as nurseries for raising its young ones. It searches out such carrots in order to lay eggs in their roots. Carrot flies are still keener on soils to which peat has been added, since they then find it easier to reach the roots and lay their eggs.

The cutworm

It is easy to get rid of the cutworm. It loves carrots whose root-collar is exposed and thus turns green. We find such carrots bitter, but the cutworm (moth larva) considers them delicious. If we take care always to cover over the root-collar of carrots, there will be far less danger of any damage.

Slugs

In some places slugs assume real plague proportions. There are people who get up at the crack of dawn and stand on guard with knives at the ready to dispatch these hated usurpers of their toil. Others catch them in quantities

and pour boiling water over them. These are methods to which people may be driven by great annoyance but which are really uncalled-for. They don't even achieve anything, for this just attracts more snails from around about to fill the vacuum. It will often take many years to re-establish a harmonious situation, with a bearable number of slugs.

Familiarising ourselves with the life and life-cycle of these creatures is the first step in finding ways of regulating them. No-one should wish to get rid of slugs altogether for they fulfil important tasks in nature. Not to mention their slime, which most gardeners know is extremely fertile.

But let us look firstly at why slugs sometimes appear in larger numbers. They are, for instance, very pleased if people water unnecessarily. They also develop and reproduce well under some kind of soil-covering, such as a moist mulch.

We have also noticed that too much chalk and uncomposted animal body

Above left: slugs are hermaphrodite. here two of them mate and exchange sperm with one another.

Left: Slug laying eggs at night.

substances (wool, bones etc.) strongly encourages slug-reproduction.

It is therefore vital to use only mature, well-rotted compost on growing beds. In addition one should allow light and air to penetrate the soil. Mulch should only be used in times of drought and must be removed once sufficient rain has fallen again. As already mentioned, we only water once, when planting out or replanting. Otherwise we leave it up to the heavens to provide the water that is needed. Only during prolonged dry periods do we try to support plants through appropriate means (see pages **66** onwards). Since slugs are tasty morsels for hedgehogs, frogs, slow-worms, lizards, chickens, ducks and other types of birds, we should encourage such wildlife in our garden. This will soon keep any potential plague in check.

Applying the horn silica preparation also curbs slug infestation. We have observed that slugs increase rapidly when the planet Mars enters constellations (Fishes, Crab and Scorpion) whose forces are mediated through the element of water.

Hedgehogs are very useful in helping us combat slugs, which are their staple diet.

Slug-spray

If all these measures are of no avail, one can make a slug-spray to combat a plague of these creatures. It is made in the following way:

When the moon is in Crab, collect 50-60 slugs and place them in a bucket which can be closed with a lid, then fill it with water. Now wait until the moon is once more in Crab, by which time the slugs will have rotted down. The liquid should be finely strained and then fine-sprayed on the soil, especially where

any grassy areas adjoin soil-beds. After this a new slug-spray should be prepared, and sprayed again a month later on the same ground. This treatment should be repeated three times at intervals of four weeks.

This is considerably more humane than strewing slugs with salt, pouring boiling water over them or slicing them in half, since only 50-60 slugs are used at a time.

Making slug-spray

Above: When the moon is in Crab place 50-60 slugs into a bucket with a closable lid, then fill it right to the top with water. Close the lid tightly so that there is no space of air left in the bucket. Below: When the moon moves in front of Crab once more, spray the liquid finely on growing plots (see text).

Another method of damage limitation

If, in spite of all these measures, you still have a pest problem, there is one further way of dealing with it. To do this however, you need to try to relate to the higher, supersensible group-soul of the particular creature that is causing you problems. By burning a small number of them, and spreading the ash at the right constellation, we turn for help to the group-soul's 'invisible hand',[7] and ask that the creatures' reproduction should be reduced to bearable amounts. We can think of this process as being similar to that in which, for example, lemmings are led by an invisible hand to kill themselves when their numbers grow too many.

It is extremely important that we do not do this in anger, for then it will have no effect. We should instead try to imbue ourselves with the great laws of existence, so that nature responds to our request.

The following is a homoeopathic method which has proved very effective. However, the instructions do need to be adhered to precisely.

Directions

First collect between 50 and 60 of the pests. It is best to put them in an egg-box, which is then burned on a wood-fire. Burning and spraying must occur at the right constellation (see table on page **94**). The wood- and pest-ash produced must then be ground in a mortar for one hour (by one person only), which dynamises it. From this activated ash an 8x dilution is made: take 1g of the ash-mixture, and put it in a closable bottle with 9ml of water, then shake it for three minutes to produce a 1x dilution. Then add 90 ml water and shake again for three minutes to produce a 2x dilution. To make the 3x dilution add another 900 ml water, and so on until you reach 8x. However, from 4x onwards we start again with a smaller quantity, since we would otherwise have to shake or stir 100,000 litres to reach 8x. (See also pages **71** onwards, where this whole process is described in more detail.)

We have found it effective to fine-spray this dilution on three consecutive evenings. In the case of plant infestations the plants themselves are sprayed, while the soil is sprayed for pests inhabiting the soil. We found that the reproduction of pests treated in this way was considerably diminished.

After four weeks - when the right constellation recurs (see table) - you can if necessary make another 8x dilution from the original 4x quantity (which can be kept for up to two years), and spray this again on three consecutive evenings.

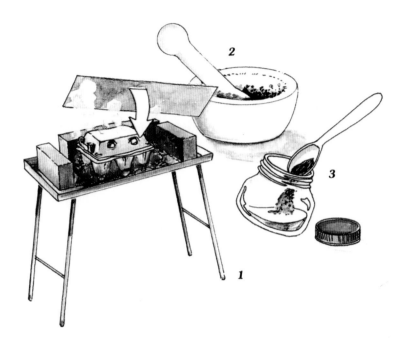

To reduce the excess reproduction of slugs it is necessary to spray all the soil in your garden three times on three consecutive evenings.

To combat excess numbers of mice, rats and other 'gnawers and nibblers' as well as birds, you will find the right constellations and times for each year in our *Sowing and Planting Calendar.* In these cases the skins or feathers of single creatures are burned.

Finally, we would like to emphasize once more that only those pests should be burned in this way which are actually causing damage on your farm or in your garden. Experienced scientists have told us that creatures specially reared for scientific trials in laboratory conditions do not give the same results.

Making an 8x dilution from burned pests to combat infestation

1. Place 50 to 60 pests of the kind you wish to combat in an egg-box. Then burn it on a wood-fire.

2. Pulverise the ash from the burned pests and the wood in a mortar for one hour (one person only).

3. From this dynamised or rhythmically treated ash make an 8x dilution (see text).

ANOTHER METHOD OF DAMAGE LIMITATION

Aphids are very familiar plant-pests.

Colorado beetles

ANIMAL PESTS

When pests should be burned, and when pest-ash or the 8x dilution should be made and sprayed:

Pest	Time
Day-flyers, such as Cabbage White, flies and midges, white fly	Sun and moon in Twins, *also* Venus and moon in Twins
Night-flyers and moths	Sun and moon in Ram, *also* Mercury in Ram
Colorado beetle, Varroa mite (pest of the bee family), Turnip gall weevil, all beetle-pests	Sun and moon in Bull
Cutworm, leatherjackets (jar worm)	Sun in Bull and moon in Scorpion
Scale insects and slugs	Moon in Crab, *also* moon and Mars in Crab
Aphids	Moon in Twins, *also* Venus in Twins
Blossom weevil	Moon and Venus in Twins
Mites, red spider mite	Venus or moon in Waterman

ROOT-PLANTS

The root-plants are all those which develop their 'fruit' in the root-region. They are sown, hoed, cultivated, harvested and preserved on root-days (see drawing on inside flap of back-cover). Exceptions to this are listed in the descriptions of individual plants which follow.

Root-plants include:

Potatoes	Garlic
Carrots	Parsnips
Radish	Beetroot
Black salsify or	Scorzonera
Celeriac	Swede
Root parsley	Onions

Potatoes also belong here, although their 'fruits' are not really roots. They

Left: Parsnip
Right: Celeriac

95

Left: Carrots which are sown and cultivated on root-days produce the best shape, yield, taste and quality.

Below: Carrots sown on leaf-days show a tendency to forked roots, which are something of a nightmare for cooks.

react very positively to root-days, both in growth and yield. Likewise onions and garlic which really belong to the leaf-plants. The following descriptions give tips and suggestions for each plant.

Carrots

Carrots should not be harvested too soon, since they then contain unripened protein: sugars are formed only at a relatively late stage. We obtained a considerable increase in quality by spraying them with horn silica preparation in the afternoon, three to four weeks before harvest when the moon was in Ram and Scales.

Carrots harvested on leaf days easily rot in storage, so this time should always be avoided.

Beetroot

The same applies to beetroot.

Beetroot can also be sown on leaf days as well as root days. We found no negative effect on their yield from doing so. Sown on leaf days, these plants, when young, gain some advantage over weeds, since they can spurt ahead of them. But for hoeing, applying horn silica preparation and harvest, root days should be chosen. Plants hoed on root days were found to have a considerably higher nitrogen content in their leaves. Since the leaves are later composted, this is a positive attribute.

If one wishes to have firm, dry beetroot, leaf days should be avoided. But if one intends to make juice from them, we recommend sowing them on root days and cultivating them on leaf days.

Celeriac

Celeriac is sown (in March) when the sun is in Fishes, and otherwise on root days.

These plants should not be sown when the sun is still in Waterman for this will later encourage them to shoot into seed.

Radishes

Radishes grown for seed should be sown when the moon is in Aries. This has a positive effect on seed-quality, and thus the following year's produce.

Radishes: some planet configurations overrule moon-zodiac influences and exert their own particular effect. By making hourly sowings we were able to observe these differences.

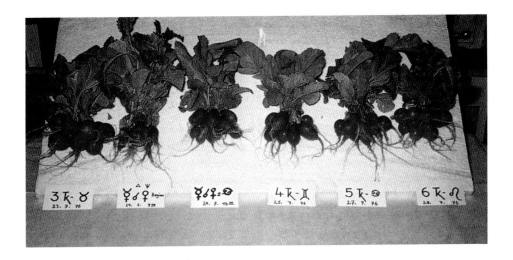

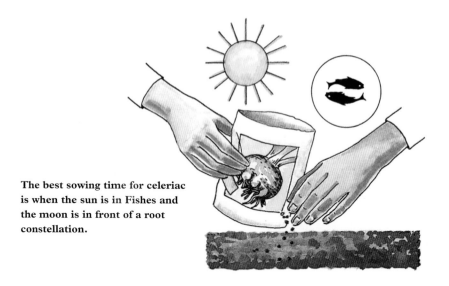

The best sowing time for celeriac is when the sun is in Fishes and the moon is in front of a root constellation.

Onions

Onions sown and hoed on leaf days produce roughly the same yield as those sown and hoed on root days. But our subsequent storage trials, in which we also included flower days, showed great differences. Leaf-day onions go bad already in early winter. Flower- and fruit-day onions begin to shoot around Christmas. Only the onions sown and harvested on root days keep for a long time - up to August of the following year. They only start putting out leaves when the sun enters Lion again.

Storing them in hay or straw also helps them keep better. It is better to fertilise them with plant compost than with dung compost - we found that they remained healthier. Dung compost attracts the onion fly and its maggots.

Garlic

Root days are easily the best time to plant garlic cloves. Autumn planting is better than spring. A good time is when the sun is in Virgin, in October.

All cultivation should if possible be carried out on root days, for this produces the best yields and storage quality.

Left above: onions

Above: garlic, a root-plant

Left below: potatoes are harvested on root days.

Potatoes

Potatoes grow healthiest and best when the soil has been fertilized in the autumn with well-rotted compost. When growing potatoes one should avoid all forcing fertilizers with a high nitrogen content.

We achieved the best results from planting potatoes on root days, hoeing them three times, and spraying them three times with silica preparation. If excessive foliage grows this should not be cut back, but one can instead spray once with silica preparation on a fruit day in the afternoon. Potatoes are ready for harvest once the foliage has died back.

is good to sprinkle them in storage with wood-ash.

For growing seed-potatoes one can just cut out the middle eyes from tubers, and plant them when the sun and moon are in Aries. These eyes

One can also cut out just the middle eyes from potatoes and plant them to grow seed-potatoes.

Potatoes planted on root days produce tubers which do not shrink and go wrinkled after harvest. Planted on leaf days they easily go rotten.

Potatoes for seed need to be planted with the moon in Ram. After harvest it

are cut out (like peeling potatoes) and planted at intervals of 10 cm. If the distances between them are any greater they grow too big and are therefore less suitable as seed.

LEAF PLANTS

These include all plants which we grow for their leaves:

Parsley
Chicory
Fennel
Most cabbages
Kohlrabi
Cauliflower (but *not* broccoli)
Swiss chard
Curly kale
All lettuces, including endives and lamb's lettuce
Asparagus
Spinach
Grass (lawn)

We did many tests with broccoli and found that it did best on flower days (see page **110**).

Leaf plants are mostly sown, planted out, hoed and cultivated on leaf days (see drawing on inside flap of back cover).

It is important to know that leaf

The savoy cabbage

days are not good times to harvest vegetables for storage, even if these are leaf vegetables. Instead one should harvest on flower or fruit days - flower days for cabbages.

Some root plants such as onions, fodder-beets and beetroot can be sown on leaf days without diminishing their yield. Beetroot sown on leaf days gain the upper hand over surrounding weeds. But onions sown on leaf days store very badly and easily go rotten.

The following gives hints about each individual type of leaf plant.

Cabbage family

All cabbage types for storing should receive their final hoeing and silica spraying, and be harvested, on flower days.

White cabbage

If you are going to make *sauerkraut* (pickled cabbage) you should choose flower days for harvesting. For sowing, hoeing and other cultivation work we recommend leaf days.

Kohlrabi

Sowing and cultivation on leaf days produces the highest yields and the best-shaped vegetables. One should avoid root days, since this can result in misshapen and sometimes scabby kohlrabi. Their taste also becomes too sharp.

For long storage in a cool place they should be harvested on flower days.

Cauliflower

Many tests have shown that leaf days are best for cauliflower. Plants cultivated on flower and fruit days start shooting before they are ripe. Such plants also produce a lower yield, though they have a nuttier

When sown on root days and moon perigee (close to the earth), cauliflower heads easily go bad.

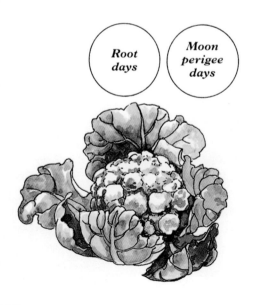

Root days

Moon perigee days

taste. Cauliflowers sown on root days quickly go bad, leaving little over for cooking.

If they are to be cool-stored for a longer period they should be harvested on flower days.

Lettuce

Leaf days should be chosen for sowing and cultivation. This considerably improves yield and quality.

Corn salad (lamb's lettuce)

Corn salad should always be sown on leaf days in spring and summer. If it is, it hardly ever shoots into seed, since all its forces are channelled into vegetative (leaf) growth. We have been able to obtain lettuce-size heads of corn salad from a single seed, which were very delicate and tasted good. For a winter or spring harvest we sow on leaf days in August.

Chicory

Although chicory is sown on leaf days, all cultivation work should be carried out on root days, so that it develops a strong root. This is harvested on leaf days and wrapped for storage. It is planted in the soil again on leaf days. If you want a quick harvest, choose days when the moon is in Fishes. If you don't

Corn salad, also known as lamb's lettuce

want to harvest until spring, then days when the moon is in Crab or Scorpion are recommended.

Spinach

Spinach grows particularly well if the soil has been pre-dressed in autumn with 1kg mature compost per square metre, for a sowing in spring. The best sowing time is when the sun is in Fishes and the moon in Fishes, Crab or Scorpion (leaf days). In the open air,

Parsley

the first hoeing takes place after about three weeks, but in the greenhouse after nine days. To produce the best crop, hoeing and spraying should be done on leaf days. Hoeing on root days gives a higher nitrogen content. Cultivation on leaf days, on the other hand, leads to a lower nitrogen content but higher sugar and iron contents, and thus a better quality of spinach.

Parsley

Leaf days are best for sowing and cultivating parsley. However if you are going to use parsley in conserves, flower days should be chosen for harvesting and preserving.

Grass (lawn)

Grass seed should be sown on leaf days. The soil is previously dressed with well-rotted compost. The seeds should be pressed into the earth since they need good contact with the soil to

104

GRASS (LAWN)

germinate. After sowing, keep the soil moist, watering in the evenings.

We recommend mowing the first time when the moon is in Crab, which helps the roots to take hold again afterwards, and leads to good, thick growth. After mowing, spray a diluted nettle liquid manure (1 litre manure to 40 litres water – see pages 45 onwards).

The grass should be fertilized with compost, when the moon is either in Crab or Scorpion.

There are two possibilities for regular mowing: if you don't have much spare time, you should choose flower days. The grass then grows less abundantly. But if you want thick grass, mowing should be carried out on leaf days; and then, of course, you will have to mow more often.

If you want your grass to grow fast and thick, mow it on leaf days (left). If you would rather get your lawn-mower out less frequently, mow on flower days (right).

Leaf days

Flower days

FLOWER PLANTS

These include all the plants whose flowers we wish to harvest; length of flowering is therefore also an important factor.

As a general rule, such plants should be sown, cultivated and harvested on flower days (see drawing on inside flap of back cover). Among them are:

Medicinal plants whose blossom is used, Broccoli, Flowers for cutting and drying, Bulb flowers, 'Preparation flowers' which we use for making bio-dynamic compost preparations (see page **41**).

Always exhilarating: a blossoming field of sunflowers.

106

Plants grown for their oils, such as sunflower or rape, also belong in some degree to the 'flower' plants. Although we get the highest yields from them by sowing on fruit and seed days, the highest oil content is produced by early morning hoeing and spraying of silica preparation on flower days. Harvesting is also best done on flower days.

There follow some hints and tips for specific plants of this group:

Rosebush beside our house: there is only 50 cm between the house and the edge of the road. In autumn we feed it with two bucketfuls of well-rotted compost and spray with the cow-pat preparation. In spring we spray with cowhorn manure; and once the leaves appear we spray them three times in the early mornings of flower days with silica preparation.

Linseed oil: clear differences in colour and oil quantity come from the different cosmic influences at work when horn silica preparation was applied.

Cut flowers

For transplanting and pricking out, flower days should be chosen, as well as for harvesting - i.e. cutting the flowers. Their scent is then most intense and the blossoms stay fresh and beautiful for longer; and the plant left growing (only the flowers are cut, not the whole plant) also puts out many new side-shoots - which leads to more blossoms and higher yields.

If cut flowers are harvested on fruit days, the remaining plant still puts out an abundance of new blossoms, but these quickly form seeds - which is not what one wants.

We found that dried flowers harvested on flower days retained their full colour and intensity, while those picked on other days soon lost theirs.

Bulbs

Bulbs are best planted on flower days in the first half of November.

Medicinal plants

Flower days should be chosen for the harvest of blossoms for making herbal and medicinal teas etc. - in other words when the moon is in Twins, Scales or Waterman.

Flower
days

Flower days

Cut flowers should be cut on flower days, which allows them to stay fresh and sweet-scented for longer. The plant left growing also puts out many new side-shoots. thus producing a higher 'yield' of blossoms.

Blossoms are dried on paper in a shady place.

Leaves of plants cultivated for their etheric oils (such as peppermint and balm (melissa), are also harvested for drying on flower days (see also the chapter on 'harvesting', pages **28** onwards).

109

Broccoli belongs to the 'flower'
plants, since it reacts so positively
to flower days.

Broccoli

Many tests have shown that broccoli likes to be treated as a 'flower' plant. Whenever light impulses (see inside flap of front cover) were active at the time of its sowing, we later harvested beautiful, firm broccoli heads. Sowing on leaf days produced a plant which put all its strength into leaf growth; while those sown on fruit days produced lots of small buds.

'Preparation' plants

We recommend the following for cultivation and harvesting of plants from which bio-dynamic preparations are made:

Dandelions should be picked in the early mornings on flower days, just after the flowers have opened. The middle of the blossom must still be closed.

Chamomile should be harvested on flower days shortly before St. John's (24 June). If you pick them later, when the blossoms have already started forming seeds, the chamomile preparation will not work properly.

Stinging nettle needs to be harvested when the first beginnings of blossom appear. The whole plant is cut off near the ground and used in the preparation.

Valerian is picked on flower days around the time of St. John's.

Dandelion or *Taraxacum officinale* is used to make one of the biodynamic preparations.

FRUIT PLANTS

These are the plants which generally respond positively to being sown, cultivated and harvested on fruit days. They include:

Beans
Strawberries
Peas
All types of grain
All types of squash, as well as courgette and cucumber
Lentils
Maize
Peppers
Rice
Tomatoes
Fruit bushes and fruit trees

When cultivating fruit plants to obtain seed, sowing, cultivation and harvest should be carried out on fruit/seed days (moon in Lion - see page **13**). This produces especially high-quality seed, better than that gained from other fruit days.

Fruit days are also particularly good for making dairy products, pickling cabbage and baking bread.

Wheat-Field. Wheat, like other grains, belongs to the 'fruit-plants'. This picture shows wheat field-trial at our farm.

Peas belong to the fruit plants.

The following are specific hints and tips for particular types of vegetable and fruit.

Peas and beans

Both of these plants produce the best yields when they are sown, cultivated and harvested on fruit or fruit/seed days.

They both belong to the *Leguminosae* family, which collect nitrogen in their root nodules. If one sows and cultivates them on root days, they produce a small yield of 'fruit', but far more root nodules, which makes them of great benefit as a green manure.

Lentils

What was said of peas and beans applies to lentils too. In trials we found that hoeing and silica spraying on fruit days considerably increases yields.

113

Tomatoes are sown, hoed and cultivated on fruit days.

Tomatoes

Tomatoes should always be sown, hoed and also cultivated on fruit days.

An almost invariable consequence of nipping off side-shoots on leaf days is fungal attack. If this work cannot be done on fruit days, flower days can be used instead.

Sowing is best done on fruit days when the sun is in Waterman.

Strawberries

If you observe wild strawberries you can see that they flower in spring before they have developed many leaves. Once fruits, then seeds, have ripened on the plant and fallen off, leaf growth becomes more copious. The flowers for the following year are prepared at the same time. In autumn the leaves go red and fall off through the winter.

We can see the same thing in our garden strawberries. To harvest sweet,

114

STRAWBERRIES

Strawberries do best when they are planted with the sun and moon in Lion.

full-flavoured strawberries, we must give them the right kind of care - which means tending them for the following year immediately after harvest. We first

Since we are close to the forest we have to protect our strawberries from birds with nets.

push the plants' tendrils back into the rows, then spread mature compost (i.e. which has become earth) between the rows, being careful not to let it touch the plants themselves. Two ten-litre bucketfuls of compost to every 10 square metres of strawberry bed are worked lightly into the surface. This should be done on fruit days when the moon is descending, during planting time in other words. Subsequently we hoe two or three times on fruit days. Following harvest, bio-dynamic gardeners give one spraying of cowhorn manure preparation on a hoeing day (fruit day) towards evening. On the next fruit day - nine days later - the cowhorn silica preparation is sprayed in the morning. This is repeated again after a further nine days, on the next fruit day. Finally, after another nine days - once more on a fruit day - the horn silica is sprayed again, in the afternoon. This process helps the plants renew themselves. All we then have to do the following spring is weed the rows, nothing else.

Strawberries grow close to the soil, to the 'fungal' level, so planting should only be done on fruit days. This will reduce susceptibility to fungal attack.

On no account should strawberry foliage be cut back, as some people recommend, for this produces fruits which go rotten.

By observing all these things you will be rewarded with a wealth of sweet, tasty, healthy fruits

Fruit bushes and fruit trees

For planting fruit trees and fruit bushes we recommend the months of October and November, once the leaves have fallen. Take care to plant on fruit days during planting time (descending moon).

November is the best time for manuring. Mature compost is applied to an area of soil corresponding to the crown. Soil organisms are still active at this time and can break down organic substances. It is important to apply the compost during planting time (descending moon). No unrotted compost should be used, since this encourages fungus and pests.

The time between mid-February and mid-March is suitable for cutting scions. Choose a fruit day and a time when the moon is in the ascendant. The scions should be stored in a cool place, wrapped in moist cloths until used for grafting. Cool cellars are good. The best time for grafting is on fruit days between the end of April and the

Above right: gooseberries, a fruit plant.

Above, far right: Blackcurrants.

Right: Apples.

Far right: Pears.

Fruit
days

beginning of May, when the moon is ascending.

Cut scions from fruit trees between the middle of February and the middle of March, when the moon is ascending. It is a good idea to cut them on fruit days.

Cut scions from fruit trees between the middle of February and the middle of March, when the moon is ascending. It is a good idea to cut them on fruit days.

A rich harvest.

FRUIT PLANTS

If you want to take cuttings from berry bushes, we recommend choosing fruit days during ascending moon. Like the fruit tree scions these are wrapped in moist cloths and stored in a cool place until March, then planted during the planting time of descending moon. (Willow cuttings are planted on flower days.) January to March is a good time to prune fruit trees, on fruit days at planting time. If there are not enough fruit days for you to finish this work, you can also use flower days.

Soft fruit harvesting is best done on fruit days during ascending moon, which keeps the fruit fresh and juicy for much longer.

Fruit for storing is best harvested on fruit or flower days. Leaf days are definitely to be avoided, for then fruit does not keep nearly so well. Fruit stores best in hay or straw.

After the fruit harvest, preferably in November during planting time, you can treat the trunks of fruit trees. Take cowdung and clay or lime in equal quantities and stir with whey until the mixture has roughly the consistency of distemper. (You can get large amounts of whey from a dairy.)Then clean the trunks and thicker branches with a wire brush and paint on with a paint brush.

If you don't manage to do this in November, it can still be done in February or March.

Fruit trees are best grafted at the end of April/beginning of May on fruit days during ascending moon.

Fruit days

APPENDIX

Resources

Cowpat preparation 'Birchpit preparation', Compost preparations, Valerian, Equisetum, Cowhorn manure and silica preparations

You can order the above products from:
Paul Van Midden, B.D. Supplies
Lorieneen, Bridge of Muchalls, Stonehaven
AB39 3RU, Scotland
01569 731746

The Biodynamic Sowing and Planting Calendar, published by Floris Books, can be obtained from:

The Biodynamic Agricultural Association
Painswick Inn Project, Gloucester Street
Stroud, GLOS GL5 1QG
Phone and fax: 01453 759 501
Email: office@biodynamic.org.uk
Website: www.biodynamic.org.uk

APPENDIX

Endnotes

1. Pages from *The Biodynamic Sowing and Planting Calendar* (published annually), by permission of Floris Books, 15 Harrison Gardens, Edinburgh, EH11 1SH

2. The English names are used rather than the Latin, to distinguish the actual constellations in the sky from the classical *signs* of astrology (tropical zodiac).

    The dates given here refer to when the sun is actually standing in front of a constellation, rather than to the 12 equal signs of the tropical zodiac. The ongoing procession of the equinoxes means that these two zodiacs (the one based on the fixed stars, and the other on the sun at the vernal equinox) have diverged from each other since the time of Ptolemy (2nd century AD).

3. 'Practical Training in Thought' from *Anthroposophy in Everyday Life*, by Rudolf Steiner. Published by Anthroposophic Press, USA, 1995, ISBN 0 88010 427 9

4. Author of *Sensitive Chaos*, Rudolf Steiner Press 1965; founder and for many years director of the 'Institut für Strömungswissenschaften' (research into water movement) in Herrichried, Germany.

5. For more information contact *Wirbela Flowforms*. UK address: Ebb and Flow, Ruskin Mill, Nailsworth, GLOS

6. *Der Technologischer Jugendfreund von 1820*

7. Rudolf Steiner described each animal's 'group-soul' as a kind of invisible hand, whose visible fingers are the separate animals belonging to it. (Translator's note.)

INDEX

INDEX

INDEX

BIODYNAMIC ASSOCIATIONS

AUSTRALIA. Biodynamic Farming & Gardening Assoc. In Australia Inc., P.O. Box 54, Bellingen, N.S.W. Australia 2454. Tel. ++61-266-55 85 51, Fax. -55 85 51. Helios Enterprises Ltd., P.O. Box 232, Northbridge, N.S.W. 2063

CANADA. Association de Biodynamic du Quebec Inc., 524 St. Joseph Quest, St. Alban, QC, GOA 3BO. Tel/fax ++ 418 268 5588.
BD Agricultural Society of British Columbia, Mr. Robert Kaird, 1434 Jefferson, West Vancouver, BC V7T 2B4.
Society for Biodynamic Farming & Gardening in Ontario, 162 Church St., Orangeville, Ontario, L9W 1P4. Tel. ++ 579 941 4525.
Canadian Biodynamic Alliance, RR-3 Marshall Road, V9L2X1, Duncan BC, CANADA,
Tel. ++1-604-7 46 41 17, Fax. -604-7 48 42 87

DENMARK. Demeterforbundet I Danmark, Victor Benixgade, 4,2., DK - 2100 København.
Demeterforbundet i Danmark, Birkum Bygade 20, Odense S, DK-5220, DENMARK Tel. ++45-65-97 30 50, Fax. -97 30 50

BRITAIN. Biodynamic Agricultural Association, Painswick Inn, Gloucester Street, Stroud, Gloucestershire GL5 1QG, Tel. ++44-1453 75 95 01, Fax. -75 95 01, Website: www.biodynamic.org.uk

EGYPT. Egyptian Bio-Dynamic Association, Heliopolis, El Horrya, P.O. Box 28 34, Kairo, EGYPT, Tel. ++20-2-2 80 79 94, Fax. -2 80 69 59, e-mail: sekem@ intouch.com

FINLAND. Biodyaaminen Yhdistys - Biodynamiska Föreningen. Uudenmaankatu 25 A, SF - 00120 Helsinki 12. Tel. ++35-89-64 41 60, Fax. -6 80 25 91

INDIA. Biodynamic Agriculture Association of India, 31 Signals Vihar, Mhow, MP 453442, INDIA, Tel. ++91-7324-7 46 64, Fax. -7324-7 31 33

IRELAND. Biodynamic Agricultural Association in Ireland, The Watergarden, Thomastown, Co. Kilkenny, Ireland. Tel. ++353 56-5 42 14, Fax. -508-7 34 24

NEW ZEALAND. The Biodynamic Farming & Gardening Assoc. in N.Z. Inc. PO Box 39045 Wellington Mail Centre. N.Z. Tel. 0-4-589 5366, Fax 0-4-589 5365.

NORWAY. Biologisk-Dynamisk Forening, Skippergt. 38, N-0154 Oslo 1.
Debio, P.O. Box 50, Björkelangen N-1940, NORWAY, Tel. ++47-63-85 63 05, Fax. -85 69 85, e-mail: kontor@debio.no

SLOVENIA. AJDA Drustvo Za Biologsko-Dinamicno Gospodarjenje, Vrzdenec 60, p, Horjul, SLO-1354, SLOVENIA, Tel. ++386-61-74 07 43, Fax. -74 07 51

SOUTH AFRICA. Biodynamic Agricultural Association of Southern Africa, PO Box 115, Paulshof ZA-2056. Tel. ++27-11-8 03 71 91, Fax -8 03 71 91.

SWEDEN. Nordisk Forskningsring, Salta, S - 15300 Järna.
Biodynamiska Föreningen, Salta, S - 15300 Järna.
Svenska-Demeterförbundet, Skillebyholm, Järna S-15391, SWEDEN,
Tel. ++46-8551-5 79 88, Fax. -8551-5 79 76

U.S.A. Biodynamic Farming & Gardening Assoc., Inc. Building 1002B, Thoreau Center, The Presidio, P.O. Box 29135, San Francisco, CA 94129 - 0135.
Tel. (415) 561-7797 Fax. (415) 561-7796.

Biodynamically grown vegetable seeds are available from: Stormy Hall Seeds, Stormy Hall Farm, Danby, Whitby, North Yorkshire, YO21 2NJ

Organic gardening resources are available in the UK from: Soil Association, Bristol House, 40-56 Victoria Street, Bristol BS1 6BY Tel: 0117 929 0661

OTHER BOOKS

Corrin, George, *Handbook on Composting and the Biodynamic Preparations*, Biodynamic Agricultural Association, Stroud, 1995

Colquhoun, Margaret & Ewald, Axel, *New Eyes for Plants*, Hawthorn Press, Stroud

Philbrick, John & Helen, Gardening for Health & Nutrition, Anthroposophic Press, New York, 1988

Soper, John (1993), *Biodynamic Gardening*, Souvenir Press, London, 1983

Schilthaus, Willy, *Biodynamic Agriculture*, Floris Books, Edinburgh, 1994

Thun, Maria, *The Biodynamic Sowing and Planting Calendar*, Floris Books

Thun, Maria (1990), *Work on the Land & the Constellations*, Lanthorn Press

These books and biodynamic preparations can be obtained from Biodynamic Associations.

Orders

Ordering information from:
Hawthorn Press
1 Lansdown Lane, Stroud, Gloucestershire
GL5 1BJ. United Kingdom
Tel: (01453) 757040   Fax: (01453) 751138
E-mail: info@hawthornpress.com
Website: **www.hawthornpress.com**

If you have difficulties ordering from a bookshop you can order direct from:
Booksource
50 Cambuslang Road, Glasgow
G32 8NB. United Kingdom
Tel: (0845) 370 0063   Fax: (0845) 370 0064
E-mail: orders@booksource.net

All Hawthorn Press Titles are available in North America from:
SteinerBooks
PO Box 960, Herndon
VA 20172-0960
U.S.A
Tel: (800) 856 8664   Fax (703) 661 1501
E-mail: service@steinerbooks.org